CW00551038

CONTENTS

ANGLESEY
AT WAR

GERAINT JONES

The
History
Press

First published 2012

The History Press
The Mill, Brimscombe Port
Stroud, Gloucestershire, GL5 2QG
www.thehistorypress.co.uk

British Library Cataloguing in Publication Data.
A catalogue record for this book is available from the British
Library.

ISBN 978 0 7524 6408 4

Typesetting and origination by The History Press
Printed in Great Britain

CHAPTER ONE

THE FIRST WORLD WAR – SETTING THE SCENE

Today, we would probably consider life in Anglesey at the beginning of the twentieth century to have been extremely primitive. Much of the population lived in poverty; for the really poor, life was a constant daily struggle. As much as 20 per cent of the population of some rural areas were dependent on some form of financial assistance provided by the parish. In 1914, the secretary of the Welsh Housing Association stated that some homes in rural Anglesey were in a far worse state than the slums of Canton in China. Many of the island's houses were damp, badly ventilated, overcrowded and were completely lacking in any sanitary facilities. Anglesey was one of the worst places in Britain for tuberculosis and other infectious diseases that are associated with poverty and lack of sanitation. School medical examinations revealed the unhealthy state of the children of the island; poor physique and tooth decay were prevalent. Children suffering from tuberculosis were sent to the Penhesgyn Open Air Home (near Menai Bridge) which was established in 1908. The Cefni Hospital at Llangefni treated adults with tuberculosis from 1915.

Without doubt, one of the factors contributing to this unhealthy state of affairs was the lack of a clean water supply in many parts of the island. Anglesey's largest town, Holyhead, had water provided by the Holyhead Water Company since the 1860s. In 1905, Llyn Traffwll (2 miles south of Bodedern) became a water reservoir for Holyhead. The Menai Bridge area was provided with water from wells near the present site of Ysgol David Hughes. Llangefni took its water from three local wells and Beaumaris took its water from Llyn Pen-y-Parc (about a mile south-west of the town). Valley obtained its water from Llyn Maelog which also served Rhosneigr. Cemaes, Benllech and Amlwch took water from rivers or wells. The provision of water throughout most of the island was very primitive indeed.

With the exception of the A5 post road (built at the beginning of the nineteenth century), the island's roads were poor and many were little better than tracks. Anglesey's three railway lines offered a much better means of travel for those living within reach of a station, especially since motor cars were the preserve of the very rich and totally beyond the means of most of the island's people.

In 1914, only three towns in Anglesey had electricity – Holyhead (operated by the Urban District Council since 1906), Llangefni and Menai Bridge. The supply was produced locally. Electricity was therefore very new and comparatively few homes in these three areas were actually connected to the supply. Gas was available only in a few urban areas and was produced locally from coal at a gas works. Telephones were virtually unheard of; most ordinary people had never used one – this being the case, communication was by letter or telegram. Post offices could receive urgent messages by telegraph and deliver them locally.

The dominant industry was agriculture and in Anglesey large numbers of agricultural labourers were employed; the wages were low, typically between 15s and £1 per week. Farms were not highly mechanised and the main motive power was the horse, as it had been for centuries.

The tourist industry, on the other hand, was in its infancy at the beginning of the twentieth century and there was a trickle of holidaymakers frequenting such resorts as Benllech, Rhosneigr and Trearddur Bay. There is evidence that some wealthy people from the English conurbations owned holiday homes in coastal areas such as Trearddur Bay; holiday homes are not a modern phenomenon. Rhosneigr railway station was built in 1907 and the line to Benllech was completed in 1909. It was hoped that both schemes would draw in holidaymakers and produce additional revenue for the LNWR railway company.

Wars were a common occurrence throughout the centuries and Britain had been involved in many of them. The nineteenth century had witnessed many conflicts, such as the Napoleonic Wars, the Crimean War and the Boer Wars. These were battles fought in distant countries with no direct impact on the civilian population at home, other than the fact that British servicemen were fighting in them. Thousands of men died in these wars. For example, in the Crimean War (1853–6), some 2,750 men were killed in action but over 16,000 died of disease. Similarly, in the Second Boer War (1899–1902), 7,900 were killed in action and over 13,000 died of disease. However, these figures pale into insignificance compared to the world wars of the twentieth century.

The assassination of Archduke Franz Ferdinand (heir to the throne of the dual kingdom of Austria-Hungary) in Sarajevo on 28 June 1914 by an Austrian subject of Serbian blood, Gavrilo Princip, is the usual reason given for the start of the First World War. Some historians regard this as an excuse for the war rather than its cause which included Austria-Hungary's ambitions in the Balkans. Furthermore, Germany had adopted an aggressive stance under Kaiser Wilhelm II and from 1898 had begun the process of enlarging its navy which could prove a threat to Britain, then the world's most powerful maritime nation. Britain had agreements with the two powers to the west and east of Germany, namely France and Russia. David Lloyd George, a minister in the Liberal Government of Henry Herbert Asquith was confident that common sense and goodwill would prevail and that any large-scale conflict could be avoided. After the assassination, however, Austria-Hungary decided to take action against Serbia which was suspected of involvement in the archduke's murder.

Within a few weeks, by reason of various treaties and agreements between countries, a full-scale war had developed throughout Europe and elsewhere and eventually involved most countries in the world to some degree. The United Kingdom (including the whole of Ireland which was at that time under British rule) and its overseas colonies, France, Russia, Serbia, Belgium, Italy and Japan (the 'Entente Powers') fought against the 'Central Powers' (Austria-Hungary, Germany, Turkey and Bulgaria).

THE HOME FRONT 1914–18

Airships

The Royal Naval Air Service (RNAS) station was located on a 242-acre site at Mona, now used as an airfield. It employed airships and aeroplanes and was active from 26 September 1915 until 1919. It had a sub-station at Malahide Castle (on the coast of County Dublin) in Ireland, and was responsible for patrolling a very large area of sea extending from Anglesey to Morecambe Bay in the east and to Dublin in the west. A substantial camp was set up in the vicinity of the airship station to house the station's personnel.

Anglesey Volunteer Reserves

The Anglesey Volunteer Reserves were formed in 1917 and men were actively recruited throughout the island. The reserves were based at the Kingsbridge camp at Llanfaes and the organisation was made up of men who were unable to enlist in the Regular Army or who claimed had exemption from conscription. There were approximately 1,200 men in the AVR, under the command of Major Hugh Pritchard of Llangefni. They performed guard duties on the Menai Suspension Bridge and the Britannia Railway Bridge as a precaution against possible sabotage linked to unrest in Ireland. There were always ten men on duty on the bridges.

Anti-War Campaigning

The anti-war monthly *Y Deyrnas* (The Realm) was published in Bangor and ran between October 1916 and November 1919. It contained articles by various religious figures and socialists and drew attention to the plight of conscientious objectors who were imprisoned and harshly treated for their beliefs. Its circulation was never particularly high, and it is said that its sales in Anglesey were disappointing. In fact, comparatively few prominent people spoke against the war, and even fewer were prepared to listen.

Army Camps

The Kingsbridge camp, near Llanfaes, had been opened in 1902 as a tented summer camp for the militia. The Anglesey militia was originally formed in 1762 and one of their functions was to quell incidents of social unrest. The militia became known as the Royal Anglesey Royal Engineers in the 1870s, and at the Kingsbridge camp were taught a number of skills including bridge-building and carpentry. The unit saw service in the Boer War of 1899–1902. In 1911 the camp started the work of training reservists as army engineers. By 1914 the camp was enlarged with permanent buildings and hundreds of troops arrived to receive specialist training – soldiers who would then be sent to France. In 2008, the *Daily Post* reported that two local archaeologists had discovered the remains of what they believed to be practice trenches at the Kingsbridge site. During the First World War, soldiers in uniform were much in evidence at the ports of Holyhead and Amlwch and the men were often billeted, by compulsion if necessary, in many Anglesey homes. The large Station Hotel at Holyhead was taken over by military personnel as an administrative centre for a time.

The Defence of the Realm Act

This Act was passed by Parliament on 8 August 1914. It gave the government wide-ranging powers, such as the right to requisition land or buildings for the war effort or to create regulations for lighting, criminal offences, censorship and so on. Certain apparently innocent activities, such as lighting bonfires and flying kites were forbidden; even feeding bread to wild animals was prohibited for a time because it was classed as a waste of food. People who were in breach of these regulations could, in principle, be sentenced to death. In Anglesey, there were many minor breaches of these regulations throughout the war and the courts were kept busy.

Hospitals

The Stanley Sailors' Hospital was established on Salt Island, Holyhead, in November 1871. A remarkable woman called Jane Henrietta Adeane (a niece of W.O. Stanley of Penrhos) had been associated with the hospital since 1881; during the war the hospital was taken over by the military and she assumed the title 'commandant'. Hundreds of patients from all over the world passed through the hospital during the course of the conflict as well as a large number of staff. Many of the nurses came from the Voluntary Aid Detachment (VAD) of the Red Cross.

Other buildings also took the role of 'hospitals' although in reality they were convalescent homes for the large number of wounded servicemen. The Assembly Rooms (Holborn Road), the Sailors' Home (Newry Beach), and Llys y Gwynt

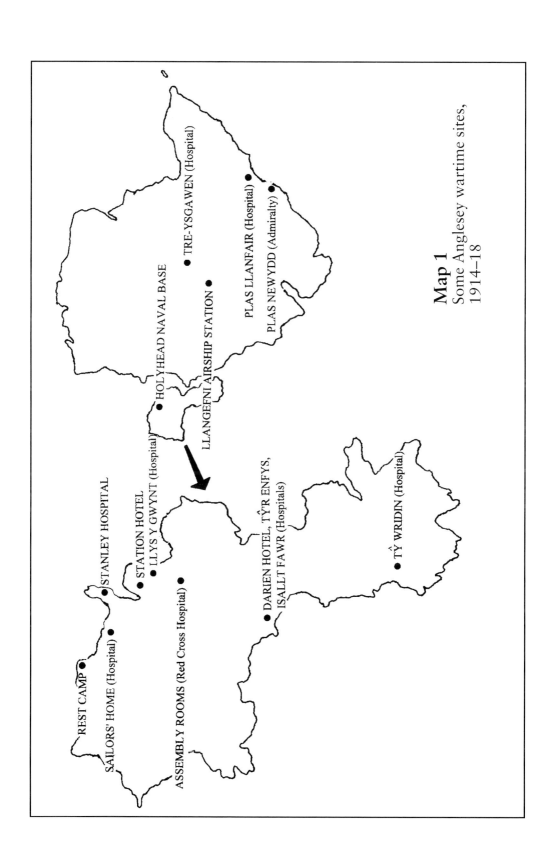

REST CAMP ●

SAILORS' HOME (Hospital) ●

STANLEY HOSPITAL ●

STATION HOTEL
LLYS Y GWYNT (Hospital) ●

ASSEMBLY ROOMS (Red Cross Hospital) ●

DARIEN HOTEL, TŶR ENFYS,
ISALLT FAWR (Hospitals) ●

TŶ WRIDIN (Hospital) ●

HOLYHEAD NAVAL BASE ●

LLANGEFNI AIRSHIP STATION ●

TRE-YSGAWEN (Hospital) ●

PLAS LLANFAIR (Hospital) ●
PLAS NEWYDD (Admiralty) ●

Map 1
Some Anglesey wartime sites,
1914–18

Tŷ'r Enfys, Trearddur Bay, was used as a hospital during the First World War.

Llys y Gwynt in Llanfawr Close, Holyhead, was also used as a hospital during the First World War. During the Second World War it was the home of a Dutch Naval Officer. The building is now used as accommodation for young homeless people.

(Llanfawr Close) all located in Holyhead, assumed this role. Isallt Fawr, Tŷ'r Enfys and the Darien Hotel (all three at Trearddur Bay) also became wartime convalescent homes, as did the Lady Thomas Convalescent Home which was opened in Holyhead a few months after the war (and later became the Gors Maternity Hospital). Tŷ Wridin, Rhoscolyn (maintained by Sir M.M. Grayson MP) was also used for a while. Much of the work at these institutions was voluntary and social events were often arranged for patients in order to aid their recovery. Elsewhere in Anglesey, Plas Llanfair (Llanfair Pwllgwyngyll) and Plas Tre-Ysgawen (Capel Coch) were also used as temporary convalescent homes. From March 1918, there was also a Rest Camp at Holyhead which could cater for 1,000 people; no fewer than 73,000 men passed through this camp during the war, including Sinn Féin prisoners such as Éamon de Valera.

Censorship

A considerable degree of censorship was imposed by the government and the press was limited in what it could print. Even so, letters written by soldiers from the trenches of the Western Front reached home and were often printed in local newspapers. A number of letters written by Anglesey servicemen would have been written in Welsh and these were also censored by the authorities.

Land Army and Agriculture

The U-boat menace caused shipping losses that made Britain more dependent on home-produced food during the First World War. Prices rose and agriculture enjoyed a period of prosperity during the war, of which the main beneficiaries were the farmers. Other working people, who struggled to scrape a living, were often resentful of the farmers' prosperity. In 1917 the Corn Production Act gave farmers guaranteed prices: good prices were obtained for milk, beef and grain crops. Anglesey's War Agricultural Committee was given a quota of 18,000 additional acres on the island, bringing the total arable area to 75,000 acres.

The Women's Land Army was formed in 1916 and by 1917, over a quarter of a million women worked as farm labourers or in the Women's Timber Corps.

Posters

About a hundred different recruitment posters were issued at the time of the First World War, the most famous of which was the Lord Kitchener poster (a national hero who became Secretary of State for War in 1914) with his moustachioed face and his pointing finger, exclaiming 'your country needs you'.

Prisoners of War

By the end of the First World War, the larger prisoner of war camps in the UK had smaller working camps or agricultural depots attached to them, and these covered quite large areas of the country. The large Frongoch camp in Merionethshire had subsidiary camps throughout Wales. In Anglesey, some German prisoners were housed in a camp near Llangaffo and many of them worked in the harvest and on drainage schemes on the Malltraeth Marshes. From 1917 extensive use began to be made of German prisoners of war for other work owing to the shortage of labour and food. Most worked in agriculture but many were also engaged in construction, road repairs, land reclamation and quarrying. Employers were charged for the use of prisoner labour at the usual local rates. The number of prisoners of war engaged in work throughout Britain is estimated to have been in the region of 100,000.

Rationing

In the first part of the war, food remained reasonably plentiful. However, German U-boats sank large numbers of ships carrying imported food and by 1917 there were shortages, particularly bread. From early 1918 a number of basic food items were rationed, including sugar, butter, margarine, cheese and meat. The public were issued with ration coupons from July 1918 and would have to register with a shop of their choice.

Refugees

About 300 Belgian refugees came to Anglesey and stayed in various places, including Menai Bridge and Amlwch. Their stay in Anglesey was comparatively short with many moving to England to seek work. During their stay, the Menai Bridge refugees helped locals to build a promenade from Carreg yr Halen, Menai Bridge, to the causeway at Church Island and it is still known to this day as the Belgian Promenade. It was badly damaged by storms in the early 1960s and was repaired in 1965, having been officially opened by Eduard Willems, the sole survivor of the original workforce.

Support and fundraising organisations

There were many organisations that made their contribution to the war effort in one form or another. Funds were collected for various charities such as the Red Cross, and War Relief Funds were established in several areas to alleviate hardship, particularly for families of servicemen. Flag days were a popular means of raising money. The government raised the vast sums needed to finance the war through the sale of War Loan Stock and various savings certificates. There was an insatiable demand for public money at a time when many of Anglesey's poor were struggling to make ends meet. Sewing and knitting groups, who made items such as socks and gloves for soldiers were busy in many villages, often being associated with a particular chapel or church. Among the more unusual organisations was one known as 'Eggs for the Wounded' in Beaumaris.

Women

An organisation known as the Voluntary Aid Detachment (VAD) came into being in 1909. Although not exclusively a women's organisation, many middle- and upper-class women, with time on their hands, performed voluntary duties, mainly in hospitals (such as those in Anglesey) as auxiliary nurses. When war broke out in 1914, there was a greatly increased demand for VAD nurses and by the end of the war tens of thousands were at work in hospitals throughout Britain and in Europe. Other women's organisations formed during the war were the Women's Royal Naval Service (WRNS, established in 1916), the Women's Royal Air Force (WRAF, formed in April 1918), the Women's Auxiliary Army Corps (formed in March 1917 to assist as clerks, cooks, drivers, telephonists, etc.) and the Women's Land Army (established in 1916). In addition, many women took over men's jobs in factories, delivered mail and even drove buses.

CHAPTER TWO

1914

It may seem surprising to us now, but when Britain entered the war on Tuesday 4 August 1914, there were street celebrations throughout the country and in most of Europe's capital cities. No one could have envisaged the appalling trench warfare and the enormous casualties that would occur. Indeed, there was a naïve expectation among many that the war would be over by Christmas. Many young men saw the war as a great adventure and flocked to enlist; so many in fact that conscription into the armed forces was unnecessary until 1916. The British Government asked for 100,000 British volunteers in August 1914, but in fact 761,000 enlisted in the first two months of the war alone. By January 1915, over one million men had volunteered. A volunteer soldier in 1914 could expect to earn 1s per day. Few of those who volunteered could have had any concept of what lay ahead of them.

In his recollections of life in the market town of Llangefni entitled *Cnoc ar y Drws* (*A Knock at the Door*), T.C. Simpson (then in his early twenties) recalls the beginning of the war. He relates how twenty naïve young men, himself included, visited the County Offices to enlist simply because they were keen to acquire a uniform like that worn by the recruiting officer. Simpson admits that they had no notions of combat whatsoever!

A contemporary of T.C. Simpson was Ifan Gruffydd (1896–1971) of Llangristiolus. In his remarkable Welsh language autobiography entitled *Gŵr o Baradwys* (*A Man from Paradise*), Ifan Gruffydd gives a memorable picture of rural Anglesey life at the beginning of the twentieth century. He maintains that Anglesey people at that time saw wars and military matters as distant and alien affairs which did not concern them. There was a widespread belief that fighting wars was England's work and that the job of the Welsh was merely to hear of their exploits. In August 1914, a recruiting sergeant in Llangefni (wearing an impressive uniform including a red coat, blue trousers, a velvet cap and spurs) persuaded Ifan Gruffydd to sign a piece of paper committing him to army service for six years.

It was easy to persuade unsophisticated rural dwellers who had limited command of the English language into signing slips of paper; many others were probably fooled in the same way. By the end of the war, it is estimated that as many as 100,000 Welsh-speaking soldiers had served in the war; a considerable number would not have been particularly fluent in English.

One of Anglesey's most prominent Presbyterian chapel ministers, the Revd Thomas Charles Williams of Menai Bridge, regarded the First World War as a 'just war' and encouraged young men to enlist.

Sir John Morris-Jones, professor of Welsh at Bangor University, lived at Llanfair Pwllgwyngyll. He also encouraged young men to sign-up.

The declaration of war caused a wave of jingoistic patriotism to sweep over the country and Anglesey was no exception. Those who spoke against the war, a few religious figures and socialists, were very small in number. Well-known local figures such as John Morris-Jones, the much respected Professor of Welsh at the University College of North Wales, Bangor (who lived in Llanfair Pwllgwyngyll) actively encouraged young men to enlist. Sir Henry Jones, the educationalist and philosopher, also campaigned to recruit soldiers. He was an eminent Welshman of his period and a friend of David Lloyd George. Respected and influential local religious figures, such as the Revd Thomas Charles Williams of Menai Bridge and the charismatic Revd John Williams of Brynsiencyn described the conflict as a 'just war'. But it was not an easy task to persuade young men who had been brought up in the chapel and had experienced the religious revival (Y Diwygiad) of 1904–5 to volunteer for war. In Anglesey, volunteers were initially comparatively few in number and many people were very critical of this slowness, which was perceived by some as unpatriotic.

Government Minister David Lloyd George (1863–1945) showed great enthusiasm for the First World War. He urged young men to enlist and was keen to establish a 'Welsh Army'.

Local newspapers devoted considerable space to their coverage of the war. The progress of the conflict in Europe received considerable attention but the work and experiences of local people was also extensively reported. *Y Clorianydd* was a 4-page weekly Welsh language paper, published on Wednesday, and costing ½d. In the 5 August issue (the first issue since war was declared) most of the usual features and mundane advertisements were unchanged; one front page advertisement proclaimed in Welsh that 'The best place in Anglesey for satisfaction for the feet is O.J. Williams' [shoe] shop at 3 Glanhwfa Road, Llangefni'. However, inside, a small paragraph told a more sinister and disturbing story, and brought the reality of war to the people of Anglesey:

> . . . the Germans have detained a British vessel, the *Saxon*, in the Kiel Canal, near Hamburg. Her master is Captain Rowland Humphreys [aged 35] of Amlwch Port, and three of the hands are also from there, W. Moulsdale [Brickpool, Amlwch Port], Harry Wynne [16 Brickpool, Amlwch Port, aged 22] and Richard Hughes [Brickfield Street, Amlwch]. The Chief Engineer is from Benllech and the Second Engineer is named E. Parry [aged 32] from Penysarn. [Translated].

The *Saxon* was a 495-ton coaster built in 1898 and owned by T.W. Smyth and Company of London. The crew were unlucky to be at the wrong place at the wrong time; their families would wait a long time to see them again. The *Saxon* was not the only vessel detained in Germany under similar circumstances; other Anglesey men also found themselves prisoners. The same issue of *Y Clorianydd* reported that prayer meetings had been held at some of the island's chapels, calling for an early and peaceful outcome to the situation.

The *Holyhead Chronicle* was an 8-page English language weekly published on Fridays, costing 1*d*. Today we would not regard these local papers as 'reader-friendly' as they were mostly set with tiny print and photographs were only rarely printed. Both the *Chronicle* and *Y Clorianydd* were written in the very formal style of the period and totally unlike their modern counterparts. A paragraph in the 7 August issue of the *Chronicle* must have summed up the feelings of many:

> It has been a strange Bank Holiday for Britain, for Europe, for the whole world; the awful shadow of the war cloud drawing nearer and nearer, the many wild rumours, the coming and the going of the Territorial troops, the mobilisation of the naval reserve; the general uncertainty and dread. And, strange to say, with one stupendous exception, we seem to be at peace with all the world, having no cause of quarrel, offensive or defensive, with any nation . . .

The same issue was keen to report 'thrilling details' of the sinking of a German minelayer, *Königin Luise*, at Harwich. She was a German passenger ship adapted for laying mines, and her destruction provided further evidence that the war at sea was already under way, with activity by both sides.

At the beginning of August, an open-air meeting was held in Victoria Square, Holyhead, to protest against the raising of food prices by certain local shopkeepers. Some traders were said to have increased their prices by as much as 100 per cent. There were suggestions that wealthier members of society had been hoarding goods and they were urged to return them to Holyhead Urban Council who would 'buy them at the prices paid for them'.

The first week of August saw a large number of railway passengers passing through Holyhead. The *Chronicle* reported that wives and children 'with tears streaming down their faces clung to husbands in passionate farewell.' In the same week, it was reported that an aeroplane was seen over Holyhead 'at a great height and travelling at a tremendous speed in the direction of Amlwch.' Aeroplanes would have been a most unusual sight in Anglesey at this time and the event was obviously considered newsworthy.

Some things went on as usual, of course. Holyhead Town Hall was screening an episode of the American film serial *Lucille Love, the Girl of Mystery* starring Grace Cunard. It was described as a 'sensational picture, which has been secured at great expense.' Incidentally, Holyhead had had a cinema since the Hippodrome opened its doors in 1909. On the other hand, the Anglesey Agricultural Show, due to be held at Llangefni on 13 August, was postponed indefinitely. The Beaumaris Sheepdog Trials suffered a similar fate.

In August the Holyhead War Relief Fund was established to care for wives and children as their husbands had left suddenly to join the war effort. There was an appeal for funds and a committee was formed. House to house collections were also organised. A fortnight later the fund is reported to have exceeded £320.

Within days of the declaration of war, the Admiralty requisitioned the four ferries (*Cambria*, *Scotia*, *Anglia* and *Hibernia*) operating from Holyhead (owned by the LNWR) and they underwent complete transformation into armed boarding steamers. The work was carried out at the Marine Yard, Holyhead, and was completed in only ten days. This is testimony to the skills and expertise which existed in Holyhead's shipyards at that time.

On Sunday 9 August, eight Germans (five men, one woman and two children) arrived at Holyhead from Ireland on the mail boat. They were detained at the local police station 'pending enquiries'. Later in August, it was reported that the Admiralty had taken up the offer of a camp at Plas Newydd from the Marquess of Anglesey. The County Theatre in Bangor (patronised by many people in southern Anglesey) boasted that it was showing 'War Pictures' which they described as 'the first in North Wales'. Colonel Dixon at Menai Bridge Recruiting Station was urging Anglesey people who owned motor cars to convey recruits to recruiting stations.

On a lighter note, the *Chronicle* reported that Miss Leely Le Feuvre (aged fifteen) of Seacombe, Wallasey, who was on holiday in Holyhead, had swum around the mailboat which was anchored near the breakwater. The 1½-mile swim took her 25 minutes.

Newspapers continued to publish advertisements for shops and other businesses in the same way as before the war although their rather formal style is very different to their present-day equivalents. Advertisements for various patent remedies were also very common, such as Beecham's Pills ('the greatest digestive medicine of our time') or Ladies Blanchard's Pills ('unrivalled for all irregularities . . . never fails to alleviate suffering').

Advertisements from a less sophisticated age often seem comical to us today. But local papers also carried some astonishingly pointless reports such as one which appeared in the *Chronicle* of 28 August:

> Mrs Roberts, 23 Stanley Street and forty friends motored out to Ellen's Tower [near South Stack] on Tuesday afternoon, where an enjoyable picnic was held.

On a more relevant note, the same edition of the *Chronicle* also printed a letter from an anonymous source urging young men to enlist:

> It is very disconcerting that so far the efforts made to enlist recruits in the County of Anglesey for the Reserve Army have for some reason or other not met with the success they demand. Possibly it may be due to the effect that young men of the county have not realised their great responsibility to their country . . . The young men of our port [Holyhead] are quite ready to attend picture shows and to cheer as they see photos of our leaders exhibited on the screens, but their cheering ends in mere empty vapour and not in any active work or service . . .

But on 2 September, it was reported that 71 young men left Holyhead railway station to join the Royal Anglesey Royal Engineers at Beaumaris. Three days later a recruitment meeting was held at Menai Bridge, where the speakers included Mr Ellis Griffith, Anglesey's MP, the Revd Thomas Charles Williams (Minister of Capel Mawr, Menai Bridge) and the Rector of Menai Bridge.

On the back page of its 2 September edition, *Y Clorianydd* proclaimed in large print, using the typical multiple headlines of the period:

TERRIBLE FIGHTING IN FRANCE
BRITISH MEN GAIN DISTINCTION
GERMANS SUFFER HEAVY LOSSES [Translated]

It was what people wanted to hear. Such headlines would create the impression that the war was progressing satisfactorily, without actually revealing very much. The 11 September edition of the *Chronicle* carried two large photographs of the destruction at Louvain in Belgium caused by the German advance, while the 16 September edition of *Y Clorianydd* printed exactly the same photographs. For the first time, perhaps, the ordinary people of Anglesey saw something of what was happening in Europe – how the conflict was being fought in the towns and villages and the effect it was having on ordinary people. In the same week, the *Chronicle* published a letter from J.R. Roberts of Llanfihangel Rectory, Llanfyllin, under the title 'Wake up Wales':

As a patriotic Welshman, I cannot disguise my keen disappointment at the very poor response which the Welsh-speaking districts have made to Lord Kitchener's appeal for men . . .

Another letter, from a person known only as 'X' appeared in the same edition under the title 'Nonconformists and Recruiting':

May I suggest through your widely read paper that each incumbent in Wales should state (1) the number of men who have volunteered for the war in his parish; (2) how many of those are Churchmen and how many are Nonconformists. This might throw some light on the teaching of Nonconformity in Wales. The parish where I am staying is a hot-bed of Nonconformity. None but Churchmen have volunteered and I hear that this is more or less general. The young men say (1) that they can get better wages at home, and (2) that they are told (by whom?) that if the Germans conquer England, they will not be affected in any way. Is this the 'Gallant little Wales'?
    Yours etc., X.

Quite a number of letters to the press, particularly in the English language *Chronicle*, seemed to have a somewhat anti-Nonconformist tone. In mid-September it was reported that 562 men had left Holyhead on active service. On Thursday 10 September a party of 42 Belgian refugees (monks and nuns) passed through Holyhead, and after being given refreshments by the ladies of the Red Cross detachment, they proceeded on their journey to Dublin on board the ferry *Rathmore*.

In mid-September it was reported that a Holyhead man, Thomas Rowlands of 7 Wynne Terrace, had been among those taken captive by the German cruiser *Dresden* 150 miles off the coast of Brazil on 15 August. German officers and crew boarded the 3,352-ton steamship *Hyades* in which Mr Rowlands served and ordered the crew into boats. The Germans then scuttled the *Hyades*. The crew of the *Hyades* arrived in Rio de Janeiro on 19 August and were then transported to Liverpool on board the *Oriana*.

The recruitment of young men into the armed forces was still proving to be a slow process in most parts of Anglesey, so as a consequence, a series of recruiting advertisements appeared in the local papers from mid-September, in English in the *Chronicle* and in Welsh in *Y Clorianydd*:

G R
FOR THOSE WHO WANT TO
serve their country
An appeal to the

Young Men of Anglesey
TO JOIN THE
ROYAL WELCH FUSILIERS

A further addition of 500,000 men to
His Majesty's Regular Army is immediately
necessary in the present grave National Emergency

TERMS OF SERVICE

General service for the period of the war only
Age on Enlistment   19-35
Ex-soldiers   19-45
Must be medically fit and height 5ft 6in
Chest measurement 35in
Separation allowance given for wives and children
Men enlisting for duration of war will
be discharged with all convenient speed
when war is over, unless they desire to remain.

HOW TO JOIN

Men wishing to join should apply to the
Police or Post Office or at the following Recruiting Offices:

Menai Bridge: Water St   Llangefni: Memorial Institute
Beaumaris: Barracks   Llannerch-y-medd: Police Station
Holyhead: 72 Market Street   Amlwch: Police Station

Colonel Dixon   Menai Bridge   Recruiting
Captain Wyatt   -do-   Officers

GOD SAVE THE KING

By the beginning of November, in an attempt to enlist more men, the height requirement had been reduced to 5ft 4in and from mid-November it had been reduced again to 5ft 3in. By January 1915 the upper age limit would be extended to 38. By the beginning of March 1915, the minimum height would be reduced to 5ft 2in and by the end of that month, it was 5ft 1in. In June 1915 the upper age limit was extended to 40.

A 'Welsh Hospital' at Netley, near Southampton, was established in October to cater for wounded Welsh servicemen. This was much reported in the local press and many local areas made collections for this hospital. The Netley hospital was a large hospital completed in 1863; the 'Welsh Military Hospital' was actually a group of huts erected behind the Netley hospital, although this was certainly not made clear in the local papers. It was reported that the people of Amlwch hoped to fund an 'Anglesey bed' in this hospital. On a more curious note, it was reported on 18 September that no football will be played in Menai Bridge while the war is in progress. In the same week *Y Clorianydd* gave readers a stirring set of multiple headlines on its back page:

THE TIDE HAS TURNED
PURSUING THE GERMANS
THOUSANDS TAKEN PRISONER
THE BELGIANS STRIKE AGAIN
RUSSIA AND ITS VICTORIOUS LEGIONS
[Translated]

It was reported on 18 September that lady members of the congregation at St Mary's Church, Beaumaris, had undertaken to make and provide suitable articles of clothing for the soldiers at the front in connection with the efforts of the Red Cross Society. A first instalment of about 100 parcels had been received at the Church Room and further instalments each fortnight.

Inevitably, reports of deaths were beginning to reach Anglesey. On 25 September it was reported that nine men on board the British auxiliary cruiser *Carmania* (a converted Cunard passenger liner) were killed in a battle with the German armed cruiser *Cap Trafalgar* which later sank. One of those killed was Richard Edward Pierce (aged 42) of Holyhead; he left a widow and eight children.

The 2 October edition of the *Chronicle* printed a letter from B. Jones, a Scoutmaster of Newborough, berating his fellow countrymen:

It makes me feel sad and very much ashamed to read how apathetic the men of Wales are in this time of national peril and danger . . . There must be something rotten in our religion if we can look unmoved, with folded arms, while others fight our battles and defend our homes. Today the nations are offered the baptism of fire: shall Wales alone refuse to be baptised with this baptism? If so, let us remember 'he that saveth his life shall lose it, and he that will lose his life shall find it.' Yours, etc.

The Revd John Williams in his military uniform pictured with Sir Henry Jones and David Lloyd George in Downing Street.

On the same evening a meeting was held at the Town Hall in Llangefni to encourage young men to enlist. The chairman of the meeting was the Revd R.J. Edwards BA (the Rector of Llangefni), with Colonel R. Stapleton-Cotton (of Plas Llwyn Onn, Llanedwen), the Revd Thomas Charles Williams MA (of Menai Bridge) and Professor John Morris-Jones (of Llanfair Pwllgwyngyll). It was reported that a good number had attended and that the speeches were all convincing. The Revd Mr Edwards read quotations from a letter he had received from his son who was serving as an officer with the gunners and had been in the midst of the action. His son was Frank Glencairn De Burgh Edwards, and only ten days after this meeting, he was killed at the age of 29.

Concerns were expressed about moral standards at Holyhead in the 9 October edition of the *Chronicle*. The Revd John Williams, Minister of Hyfrydle Chapel, wrote:

> Each week the best and most respectable people of the town congregate at intercessory prayer meetings, but many of our young people are quite frivolous – the homes where worthy citizens should be trained are forsaken for the streets and their frivolity. It is said by those whose duties call them out late at night, that very young girls are out in the streets at almost every hour of the night. Surely this cannot be commended? They place themselves in the very path of temptation. Where is the care of the father and of the mother? Is it possible that parents can go to rest at night when their girls are out in the streets at unreasonable hours?

A great responsibility rests upon the parents . . . It is surprising that such a number of young people are out at night when they should be in bed. By doing so they are (though perhaps unknowingly) injuring themselves from the point of view of health, and it is a reflection upon the character of the home life. . .

The same topic was aired in Y *Clorianydd* during the same week, where a letter proclaimed:

. . . it is obvious enough that young people spend far too much time walking the streets and it is unfortunate to hear that a large number of young women have fallen into such bad habits and were out far too late at night. There cannot be two opinions on that. [Translated]

Increasing numbers of German prisoners were arriving in Britain and finding suitable places to hold them was proving to be a problem. It was pointed out in Holyhead that the unused sheds and yards at the Breakwater would make ideal accommodation for prisoners and Salt Island could also be used and could be 'surrounded by barbed wire'. On 9 October the *Chronicle* reported that local seaman, Henry David Jones (aged 25) of 30 Cecil Street, Holyhead, was killed when a German torpedo sank the British cruisers, *Cressy*, *Hogue* and *Aboukir* off the coast of the Netherlands. The three ships were sunk within a period of less than an hour on 22 September with the loss of 1,400 men.

In October 1914 the monthly meeting of the Calvinistic Methodists (Presbyterians), the strongest Nonconformist religious denomination in Anglesey, was held in Tŷ Mawr Chapel at Capel Coch. The Revd John Williams was certain that the Nonconformist denominations should show strong support for young men to enlist. Although not everyone at the meeting was in agreement, a clear majority supported the views of the Revd Mr Williams that the chapels should encourage young men to volunteer.

Anglesey had been touched by a distant conflict at the turn of the century in the form of the Second Boer War (October 1899 – May 1902) and the Royal Anglesey Royal Engineers had been involved in this conflict. One who took an active part in the Boer War was Colonel Owen Thomas (1858–1923), an affluent farmer and businessman. At the beginning of the war, he became the chief recruiting officer for Anglesey and shared a platform at numerous recruitment meetings with prominent local figures such as the Revd John Williams.

Owen Thomas, one of eleven children, was an unusual figure. Born at Carrog, near Cemaes, and a product of a Nonconformist Welsh rural society, in 1887 he married an English heiress, Frederica Wilhelmina Skelton Pershouse, whom he met when she was holidaying at Cemaes. She was the daughter of Mr Frederic Pershouse of Bowden, Cheshire. Owen Thomas became an authority on agriculture, and acted on behalf of the British Government inspecting land in South and East Africa for the purpose of colonisation. He enjoyed extensive contacts with important figures in the world of politics and business at an international level. But he had not forgotten his roots.

Charismatic government minister David Lloyd George, who had a considerable following in Wales, realised that he could use respected Nonconformist preachers like the Revd John Williams as a catalyst for recruitment so that a Welsh regiment could be created. In a speech delivered before an audience of London Welshmen, Lloyd George proclaimed:

> I should like to see a Welsh Army in the field. I should like to see the race who faced the Normans for hundreds of years in their struggle for freedom, the race that helped to win the battle of Crècy, the race that fought for a generation against the greatest captain in Europe – I should like to see that race give a good taste of its quality in this struggle. And they are going to do it.

Lloyd George used his influence and arranged for Owen Thomas to be made a Brigadier-General and for the Revd John Williams to be an honorary chaplain with the rank of colonel. The Revd John Williams often preached from the pulpit dressed in his military uniform, although not everyone regarded this as acceptable. Owen Thomas and the Revd Mr Williams toured the length and breadth of Anglesey and beyond on a mission to exert as much pressure as possible to recruit young men for the Army. Both men promised that they would accompany the volunteers to France. Ultimately the campaign was to prove reasonably successful.

As the result of the German invasion of Belgium, a substantial number of Belgian refugees arrived in Britain. A number of them arrived in Anglesey at various times between 1914 and 1916 – mostly at Menai Bridge, Beaumaris, Amlwch, Llangefni, Gwalchmai and Dwyran. Sixty-three refugees arrived in Menai Bridge on 12 October and were welcomed by the town's brass band which played the Belgian national anthem. It was reported that three houses in Menai Bridge had been furnished for Belgian refugees and a fourth home was proposed in Nant Terrace. Twenty refugees arrived in Beaumaris on Wednesday 14 October and were entertained by the Clio brass band. They were accommodated at the YWCA home. The *Chronicle* reported:

> The Belgians were entertained in the pier pavilion on Tuesday 20 October with animated pictures shown by a Mr Ferguson while Miss Elsie Williams and Mr J.E. Jones sang, accompanied by Miss Sophie Williams.
> The following notice has been placed in the window of the houses tenanted by the refugees 'Please don't "treat" the Belgians to drink. Every penny we can spare must be devoted to provide necessaries for the thousands who are coming to us from Belgium.'

In relation to Belgian refugees, on 16 October the *Chronicle* reported a meeting of Menai Bridge Town Council. As the clerk was reading a letter in Welsh regarding a proposed water reservoir scheme (which had to be shelved through lack of funds in 1915), town councillor Mr Samuel Parker Bidder interjected 'amid laughter' with the

Belgian refugees in Menai Bridge were housed in Nant Terrace.

remark 'Is it Belgian?' Was there really a Menai Bridge town councillor who didn't know the difference between Welsh and 'Belgian'?

On 19 October, the First Battle of Ypres began in Belgium. The battle, which ended on 21 November, was primarily between German and British troops. Almost 8,000 British soldiers died; 29,500 were wounded and nearly 18,000 men were recorded as 'missing'.

As a result of the war, the prices of many commodities, such as clothes and leather goods, had increased markedly. *Y Clorianydd* carried this apology from one of its regular advertisers, O.J. Williams' shoe shop in Glanhwfa Road:

> It is now known to everyone that because of the circumstances arising from the war and for other reasons that the price of all types of shoes is higher than ever. We assure you that this brings no profit at all to local traders. The increased prices can be attributed entirely to the fact the manufacturer has to pay a higher price for the raw materials. [Translated]

The Menai Bridge Fair (Ffair y Borth) was held as usual on 24 October. Owing to good weather, it was well-attended. One *Chronicle* reader noted that the fair had a distinctly different feel – the traditional practice of selling horses on the streets had almost ended. The Belgian refugees in Menai Bridge attracted some interest among the locals.

On Tuesday 27 October, fifty wounded Belgians arrived at Holyhead railway station and were given a 'tremendous reception' by a large crowd. They were sent for treatment and recuperation at Red Cross Auxiliary Hospital, Holyhead, and the Darien Hotel, Trearddur Bay. Also in October, Mrs Davies of the well-known Treborth family suggested that work could be provided for the male Belgian refugees in the Menai Bridge area by improving the road on the shore from Carreg yr Halen to Church Island. Funding was secured from the Belgian Refugee Fund and the work was able to proceed.

On Tuesday 3 November a further party of Belgians arrived in Anglesey, this time in Amlwch where they were given a 'hearty welcome'. They were reported to be staying at Llaingam (Llaneilian) and Ling Crag (Amlwch). In the same week, work began at the site of a new sanatorium, situated near the old windmill at Llangefni. This site was chosen because of its central location on the island and because Llangefni had an electricity supply.

On 10 November, the funeral of Major W. Griffith Phibbs of Pencraig, Llangefni, who died in action, was held at the Parish Church, Llangefni. Soldiers formed two rows as an escort from the church to the cemetery, and after the service there they fired three shots over the grave while a bugler sounded the 'last post'. Many Anglesey people were shocked by this type of military display at funerals of the fallen; it was not part of the tradition of ordinary Welsh people.

Another practice that became common during the war was the reading of Sunday newspapers. Welsh Nonconformists had never been very keen to buy such papers; chapel ministers and elders had always tended to frown on them. However, reading the *News of the World* and other Sunday papers was considered to be the best way to read the latest news about the war.

On 17 November, David Lloyd George, Chancellor of the Exchequer, introduced his first war budget. One of the budget measures was to encourage the public to invest in government securities in order to finance the war. A massive £350,000,000 of War Loan stock was issued, paying interest at 3.5 per cent and redeemable in 10–14 years. At the same time income tax was raised, and the price of beer and tea were increased.

The slow rate at which Anglesey men were volunteering for war service was clearly still infuriating some people. In the 18 November edition of *Y Clorianydd*, someone calling himself HenŴr (Old Man), left the readers in no doubt where he stood on the matter:

Young men of Anglesey, Please permit a few words from an old man, concerning my opinion of your cowardly behaviour in keeping out of the British Army at this most serious time in its history. You can make as many excuses as you like, but every reasonable, honest man thinks you are vile and unpatriotic cowards. You are no better than those German spies. You have drunk too much tea and too little healthy milk, and eaten far too much white bread and sweet cakes and far too little barley bread, porridge, bacon etc. That was the food of your fathers and grandfathers and they were men like lions. [Translated]

In the 25 November edition of *Y Clorianydd*, a letter from a reader calling himself NON.COM. drew attention to a rather unusual idea:

. . . Seeing the great need for men to enlist in the army and the fact that so many have refused to respond, even though they are physically suitable, a gentleman from Birkenhead is forming a regiment of short men and calling it 'The Bantam Brigade' and we understand that hundreds have already enlisted . . . After seeing scores of tall, strong, sprightly young men walking the streets of Llangefni and Holyhead during the hiring fairs [for farm labourers] and showing no signs of enlisting, I believe it is high time to start a 'Bantam Brigade' in Anglesey and hundreds would enlist. [Translated].

The gentleman advocating such a regiment was the rather inappropriately named Mr Alfred Bigland, MP for Birkenhead. In fact, advertisements calling for volunteers for such a regiment were to be published in Anglesey's local papers in 1915.

On Saturday 28 November, a Holyhead man was arrested and brought before magistrates on a most unusual charge. Thomas Owen Marshall of Craigydon, Walthew

Walthew Avenue, Holyhead. At the end of 1914, one of the residents of this street was charged with sending a Morse code message (by means of a light) out to sea, which was in contravention of the Defence of the Realm Act (1914).

Avenue, was charged with sending (by means of a light) a Morse code message to a person or persons unknown. Sentries on duty outside the Sailors' Home noticed that a message was being transmitted from Marshall's house. In court, Marshall alleged he was sending the message to his wife's uncle, Robert Williams, who was on a ship called the *Suffolk* which Marshall knew would be passing. The message was to the effect that 'Aunt Kate' had been at Marshall's house that evening. The accused was intensively questioned in the court. One of the questions he was asked was 'There is no German blood in the family?' to which Marshall replied, 'No, none at all.'

Thomas Marshall was remanded until Friday 4 December on bail totalling £600. When he appeared on this date, he was charged with a breach of the Defence of the Realm Act (1914). Under this Act and its subsequent regulations, no one should display any light that would serve as a signal. The magistrates fined him £10 including costs.

Early December saw a few days of very stormy weather, and the Menai Suspension Bridge was reported to have been damaged, the centre span having 'moved six inches out of place.' Traffic was prevented from using it for a short time.

By early December 1914, the Belgian refugees in the Menai Bridge area were reported to be receiving English lessons from a Mr T.J. Williams of St Paul's School, Bangor. Mr Williams was said to be using the 'direct method'. One family of Belgian refugees at Menai Bridge decided to leave and return to their farm in Malines. Also in December Belgians were reported to be encamped at Llangefni.

Also in early December almost 400 men were engaged in training for the Royal Anglesey Royal Engineers at Llanfaes. Those who could not be accommodated in the camp were billeted in private homes. At Aberffraw, ladies were engaged in sewing classes and were busily making articles for soldiers and Belgian refugees. In the same week, L.E. Fox-Pitt, of Presaddfed near Bodedern, launched an appeal (a 'shilling fund') in order to provide Christmas presents for the men who volunteered. The Christmas present was to include a New Testament bound in khaki and a bar of chocolate among other items.

The 9 December issue of *Y Clorianydd* printed a small paragraph containing some details of a communication received from a prisoner of war in Germany – Gwilym Gabriel Roberts (aged 26) of Holyhead:

KRIEGSGEFANGENENSENDUNG. Mr G.G. Roberts writes from this unpronounceable place: 'I do not know where I am, but I know I am somewhere near Berlin. It is very cold and is expected to become colder.' Mr Roberts was an officer on the *City of Cadiz* and he was most unfortunate in reaching Hamburg a few days before the war began. [Translated].

The editor of *Y Clorianydd* did not seem to realise that Kriegsgefangenensendung actually means 'prisoner of war mail' and is not a place name! Gwilym Roberts was actually held at an internment camp at Ruhleben, near Berlin.

The newspapers were also prone to printing jingoistic propaganda which occasionally verged on the ridiculous, such as this paragraph from *Y Clorianydd* in December:

> We see that some schools are starting to turn away from playing football. It is too similar to the German way of warfare . . . There is much of the German spirit in the game; a spirit of danger, selfishness and bragging, and the boys fear not being so foolish in case they are accused of being cowards; and then the game goes from bad to worse until it is no longer a game. [Translated]

By 11 December, the total number of Holyhead men killed in the conflict had reached seven. An advertisement on the front page of the *Chronicle* proclaimed that Santa Claus had arrived at Bradley's Bazaar, Holyhead. In Newborough, wealthy businessman Sir John Prichard-Jones (who had provided the village with the institute building that bears his name in 1905) had remembered the poor of his native parish and had arranged for the distribution of coal among a hundred of the most needy.

Another curious case came before the Anglesey authorities just before Christmas. It concerned a man called William Jacob Fox Kalvin (described as an optician of Rhosgaer Terrace, Gaerwen). He faced charges under the Aliens Registration Act (1914). On 14 August 1914, Kalvin had claimed that he was a Romanian, born in Bucharest on 10 November 1866, who had reached Britain in 1887 and had lived in Anglesey for 18 years. The authorities, however, had reason to suspect that he was a Hungarian, and therefore would be classed as an 'alien'. The case could not be proven and was dismissed by the court.

On Christmas Day 1914, a strange event took place somewhere in the trenches of Europe. The story was related by Private R. Leslie of the Royal Welch Fusiliers in a letter to a friend in Holyhead. The details were published in the *Chronicle*:

> . . . we had a nice and quiet time of it on Christmas Day as towards noon some of our men risked their lives to meet some of the enemy. When the other troops who were in the trenches saw that they (the Germans) were acting in a friendly way, they all did the same . . . The men began to shake hands and exchange cigarettes and all kinds of articles which could be taken home as souvenirs after the great battle is over.

CHAPTER THREE

1915

In 1915 Holyhead became a naval base with a Hunting Flotilla of destroyers and motor launches. It was initially under the command of Captain A.R. Raby RN and it covered 3,000 square miles of sea. The base had offices next to Holyhead's main post office, but was later transferred to Bryn y Môr (owned by the LNWR). The principal anti-submarine vessels used were destroyers, motor launches and adapted trawlers.

On 19 January 1915, Great Yarmouth and King's Lynn in Norfolk were attacked by German Zeppelins, while further attacks by Zeppelins followed throughout the spring of 1915. The civilian casualties caused a massive outcry and were universally condemned by the press. The Zeppelins never ventured to the west of Britain and so fortunately they were never a threat to Anglesey and the rest of Wales.

On 20 January 1915 it was reported that three beds with an Anglesey connection had been secured at the Welsh Hospital at Netley. They were named the Menai Bed, the Plas Newydd Bed and the Anglesey Bed and were realised through local fundraising. Just two days later, on 22 January, the local papers published an appeal for race, field and stalking glasses (binoculars) for the use of officers and non-commissioned officers who were being sent to the front.

Towards the end of January, it was reported that the *Leinster* had been pursued by a U-boat, thought to have been U-21. However, the *Leinster* was capable of 25mph but the U-boat could only manage 17mph and thus the *Leinster* reached her destination safely.

A public meeting was held in Holyhead at the beginning of February to discuss the question of Belgian refugees. It was claimed that there were no suitable houses for them in the town. A fear was also expressed that German spies might be masquerading as Belgian refugees and that they could be drawn to Holyhead to gather intelligence about naval activity. A few weeks later, the Admiralty announced that it would not sanction the housing of Belgian refugees in Holyhead for security reasons. Another Belgian family arrived in Anglesey at this time and was housed at Gwalchmai.

On 4 February Germany declared 'unrestricted submarine warfare' against Allied and neutral vessels and this resulted in a great increase in the number of vessels sunk by U-boats (from 3 in 1914 to 396 in 1915).

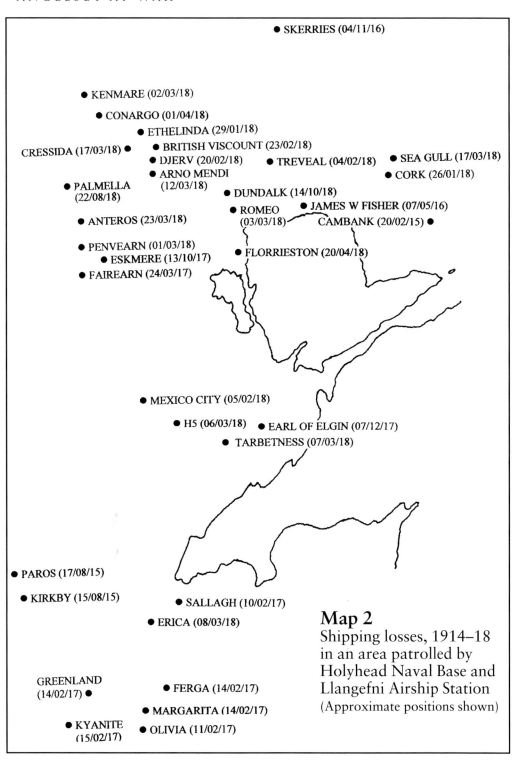

● SKERRIES (04/11/16)

● KENMARE (02/03/18)

● CONARGO (01/04/18)

● ETHELINDA (29/01/18)

CRESSIDA (17/03/18) ●   ● BRITISH VISCOUNT (23/02/18)

● DJERV (20/02/18)   ● TREVEAL (04/02/18)   ● SEA GULL (17/03/18)

● ARNO MENDI   ● CORK (26/01/18)

● PALMELLA   (12/03/18)

(22/08/18)   ● DUNDALK (14/10/18)

● ROMEO   ● JAMES W FISHER (07/05/16)

● ANTEROS (23/03/18)   (03/03/18)   CAMBANK (20/02/15) ●

● PENVEARN (01/03/18)

● ESKMERE (13/10/17)   ● FLORRIESTON (20/04/18)

● FAIREARN (24/03/17)

● MEXICO CITY (05/02/18)

● H5 (06/03/18)   ● EARL OF ELGIN (07/12/17)

● TARBETNESS (07/03/18)

● PAROS (17/08/15)

● KIRKBY (15/08/15)   ● SALLAGH (10/02/17)

● ERICA (08/03/18)

Map 2
Shipping losses, 1914–18
in an area patrolled by
Holyhead Naval Base and
Llangefni Airship Station
(Approximate positions shown)

GREENLAND
(14/02/17) ●   ● FERGA (14/02/17)

● MARGARITA (14/02/17)

● KYANITE   ● OLIVIA (11/02/17)
(15/02/17)

In February 1915, recruitment officer Owen Thomas praised the response in Anglesey. Most of those who volunteered had joined the 14th (Anglesey and Caernarfonshire) Battalion, but there still remained a considerable number of Anglesey's young men who had not enlisted.

Also in February, tragedy struck the village of Moelfre with the news that five local men had been lost at sea. They were among the crew of the 383-ton vessel *Gertrude*, on a voyage from Ellesmere Port to Waterford, which was in collision with the 4,682-ton liner *City of Vienna* not far from the Fastnet Lighthouse. Neither ship was showing any lights because of wartime lighting restrictions. The dead were named as Captain Owen Jones and his brother David, Hugh P. Jones (their cousin), William H. Jones and John Owen (of Benllech, but originally from Moelfre).

On 20 February 1915, the 3,112-ton *Cambank* (built in 1899 and en route from from Huelva, Spain, to Garston with a cargo of copper ore) was torpedoed and sunk by U-30 about 10 miles east of Point Lynas. The explosion was said to have been clearly heard on shore. Four members of the crew died, but 21 others were rescued by the Bull Bay Lifeboat. This made the people of Anglesey realise that the war was coming ever closer to them and that death and destruction were taking place in the seas around their island.

The authorities announced that there was to be a military recruitment campaign (involving 160 soldiers from the 1st Brigade of the Welsh Army Corps) throughout Anglesey lasting a whole week: from Monday 22 February to Saturday 27 February. The soldiers arrived at Menai Bridge by train from their base at Llandudno. Their itinerary and activities were widely reported in the press.

Throughout 1915 many Anglesey women continued to be fully occupied making articles for soldiers at the front. At the end of February, for example, the 6th Battalion, the Royal Welch Fusiliers (Territorial Reserve) received 60 mufflers from the Girls' Friendly Society knitting class in Holyhead.

On 28 February David Lloyd George arrived in Bangor and gave a speech at the County Theatre, which was attended by hundreds of people. *Y Clorianydd* commented:

It was said by some that he was being rather pessimistic when he said that the war would not be over until Christmas.
[Translated].

On 1 March 1915 (St David's Day), Brigadier-General Owen Thomas was presented with a Sword of Honour by Lady Boston of the Anglesey Ladies Recruiting Committee on Llandudno promenade. By this time he had recruited about 10,000 men for the 38th (Welsh) Division based at Llandudno under his command. At the beginning of March, enlistment advertisements published in local papers mentioned that a 'Bantam Regiment' was being created and that men between 5ft and 5ft 2in were being sought.

Later in March 1915, Brigadier-General Owen Thomas claimed that there were about a thousand young Anglesey men who had not enlisted, and that he was looking forward to welcoming them to Llandudno as soon as possible. *Y Clorianydd* published a letter from a soldier using the bardic name Myfyr Môn (in reality, Private R. Rowlands, based at the Llandudno camp) who painted a rather attractive picture of life in the army and at the Llandudno camp in particular:

> . . . It is not possible to lead a more comfortable life than the military life. All the officers at Llandudno are Welshmen, and they and the men are in perfect harmony together . . .
> [Translated]

By way of bringing the reader back to reality, in direct contrast, on the very same page, there was a report that 520 officers had been killed, injured or were missing in one week of warfare. When soldiers left Kinmel Park they often found themselves among English companies. The Revd John Williams discovered that Welsh soldiers in camps at Litherland and Sniggeries (near Bootle) were prohibited from speaking Welsh. Moreover, Welsh soldiers who attended Nonconformist religious services were subject to ridicule and verbal abuse by some officers. The Revd John Williams travelled there to address these issues, and despite initial reluctance by the military, matters were eventually rectified. No doubt the Revd Mr Williams' connection with Lloyd George would have had some influence on the matter.

The return of wounded soldiers from the front became a common occurrence throughout Britain. In mid-March 1915, 55 wounded soldiers arrived at Holyhead by train. They were taken to the Beach Hospital, the Stanley Hospital and one of the Trearddur Bay hospitals.

On 26 March the *Chronicle* published a letter from Corporal George Davies of Cae Mawr, Holyhead, who sounded fairly optimistic of an early end to hostilities:

> . . . I am glad to say things are going on all right and news still keeps good. We heard good news of the brave Belgian Army lately. They are doing a lot of good work up in the trenches. But there is one thing I must say about them. They are a nice set of people. They would give you anything, poor souls. They would share their last crust with you . . . I don't think this great struggle will last much longer. I think we ought to be home about the end of May, but, of course, that is my opinion. . . .

By April 1915 there was a great deal of activity both at home and overseas. On 22 April the Second Battle of Ypres began. It lasted until 24 May and it was notable for the first large-scale use of poison gas (chlorine) in warfare by the Germans. Elsewhere, on 25 April, Allied forces landed at Gallipoli in an attempt to force Turkey out of the war. The campaign was not a success and by the end of 1915 they were evacuated from the region. Both sides suffered huge casualties. Back in the UK, on 29 April, Lloyd George announced the government's scheme for regulating alcohol aimed at reducing drunkenness and absenteeism among munitions workers.

On 7 May, the ocean liner *Lusitania* was sunk by the German submarine U-20. No fewer than 1,198 people lost their lives, 124 of them being Americans. This caused great indignation in the USA and was one of the factors that would eventually bring the Americans into the war. One of those who died was a Mrs Howdle, daughter of Mr and Mrs William Hughes, Pantysaer, Tynygongl, who worked on board the ship as a stewardess. On the same day and in almost exactly the same location, the 132-ton *Earl of Lathom* (on a voyage from Connah's Quay to Limerick) was sunk; it is believed that the same submarine was responsible for both attacks. The captain of the *Earl of Lathom* was Captain Thomas Jones of Moelfre and fortunately the crew of the *Earl of Lathom* survived the attack.

On Sunday 9 May, two men from the Kingsbridge camp at Llanfaes had drowned near Beaumaris after a small sailing boat capsized. They were named as Sappers Hemaway and Hill. Two others survived the accident. A few days later the Kingsbridge camp held a sports day which was blessed by fine weather and judged to be an 'unqualified success'. In addition to the usual athletic competitions, soldiers partook of less serious activities, including a three-legged race, tug of war and 'tilting a bucket'.

On 12 May, there were anti-German riots in various parts of Britain. It was the sinking of the *Lusitania* that was at least partly responsible for this unrest. Two days later, the government began the internment of 'enemy aliens' and two large camps on the Isle of Man were used for this purpose.

At the end of May it was reported that one of the men from the *Saxon* held at Hamburg at the beginning of the war had been freed earlier in the month. He was 56-year-old Frank Green of Cardiff who suffered from rheumatism. The master of the *Saxon* was Captain Rowland Humphreys of Amlwch Port; he and the other Anglesey members of the crew remained at Ruhleben in Germany. Frank Green said:

> The officers treated us quite well but prisoners were abused by the soldiers who guarded them. Captain Humphreys protested when the guards struck some men and he was also struck. Things are better now at Ruhleben, but at first we slept above stables without beds. [Translated].

Y Clorianydd reported that Captain Humphreys had sent a message to local man Captain Robert Pritchard (of the *Pansy*) about two months earlier and that the latter had sent him eight pounds of cakes. Another of the crew of the *Saxon*, Richard Hughes of Brickfield Street, Amlwch, was released in December 1915. The internment camp at Ruhleben (then a small village 10 miles west of Berlin) was used to hold Merchant Navy prisoners as well as civilian prisoners (in other words, British people who happened to be in Germany when war broke out). Before the war, it was a racecourse. It is interesting to note that allowances were paid to the dependents of interned men.

At the beginning of June, the Revd T. Edwin Jones, the vicar of St Seiriol's Church, wrote to the Clerk of Holyhead Council to complain that the electric current supplied to St Seiriol's Church on Sunday mornings was insufficient to operate the organ. At a subsequent council meeting, it was 'resolved that the Electrical Engineer should run the Diesel oil engine on Sunday mornings so as to supply the necessary current'. This suggests that Holyhead's electricity system at this time was rather primitive.

Also in June, the Women's Institute established its first branch in Britain in Llanfair Pwllgwyngyll – the origins of the organisation being in Canada. The meeting was held at a house called Graig and was convened by Colonel R. Stapleton-Cotton of Llanedwen. The colonel, a relative of the Marquess of Anglesey, had been involved with various Anglesey ventures such as the Newborough Mat-makers' Association, an egg-collecting depot and a bacon factory (both at Llanfair Pwllgwyngyll).

In June the stark reality of the true nature of the war was becoming apparent. On 9 June, Asquith revealed that 50,342 men had died in the 7-week period between 11 April and 31 May 1915. As Y Clorianydd rightly pointed out, this figure was equal to the total population of Anglesey.

On 23 June, the new tuberculosis hospital was opened at Llangefni (at the eastern end of the town, near the old windmill). It was built by a firm of London contractors. It was described as being 180ft in length and having 24 beds. Equipped with luxuries such as central heating and electricity, it was officially opened by Lady Williams-Bulkeley of Baron Hill.

On 29 June, the National Registration Bill provided for the registration of all people aged 15–65 in Wales, England and Scotland. This was effectively a 'mini-census' of the population and could provide information that would be useful if conscription into the army became necessary.

At the end of June, the Anglesey Congregationalists held their quarterly meeting at Amlwch. Considerable disquiet was expressed concerning attendances at Sunday Schools; the meeting heard that 26 fewer teachers were available because of the war. A resolution was adopted calling for the prohibition of alcohol during the period of the war. Another resolution stated 'that the conference of the Anglesey Congregationalists rejoices to find that so many men from the county have so nobly responded to the call of King and Country in this supreme crisis in our history.'

In summer 1915 work began on the Llangefni Royal Naval Airship Station on the site now occupied by Mona Airfield. Hedges were removed from agricultural land and various buildings were constructed. These included a large airship shed (97 metres by 35 metres), workshops, gas production sheds and huts for accommodation. The station was built by the Admiralty to provide airships adapted for sea patrol as a deterrent to enemy U-boats operating in the Irish Sea, which casued massive losses to shipping.

In July, the local papers published a letter from the Llangefni Free Church Council suggesting that the last Sunday in July or the first Sunday in August be declared a 'day of submission' to mark the anniversary of the beginning of the war.

On 8 July, as the result of the massive casualties on the battlefields of Europe, Lord Kitchener made an appeal for more recruits; Walter Hume Long (of the Local Government Board) stated that the conscription of men into the Army could not be

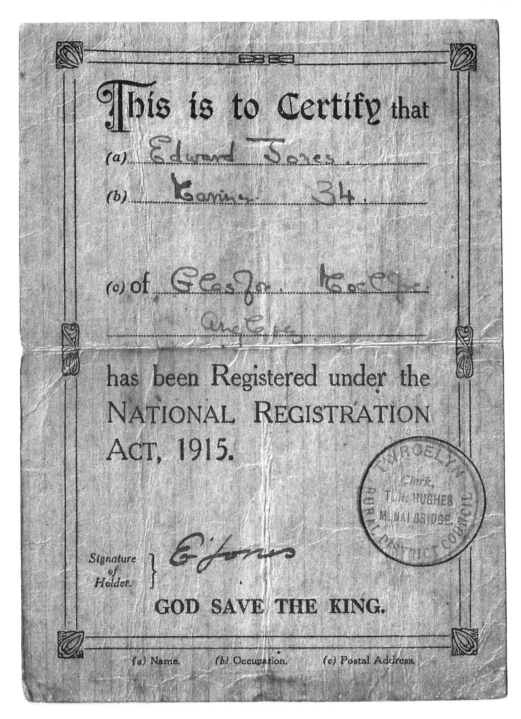

This is to Certify that

(a) Edward Jones

(b) Farmer 34.

(c) of Glasfor Kocey
Anglesey

has been Registered under the NATIONAL REGISTRATION ACT, 1915.

TWROELYN
Clerk,
T.H. HUGHES
MENAI BRIDGE
RURAL DISTRICT COUNCIL

Signature
of
Holder. E. Jones

GOD SAVE THE KING.

(a) Name.   (b) Occupation.   (c) Postal Address.

An example of a First World War National Registration document, belonging to Mr Edward Jones of Moelfre.

ruled out. Clearly, the already completed National Registration process would make the implementation of conscription easier.

On 9 July, the Tŷ Wridin Convalescent Home was opened in a country location near Holyhead. It cared for discharged sailors and soldiers and was established by a Mr and Mrs Grayson.

On 12 July, survivors of the sinking of the Glasgow steamer *Meadowfield* arrived at Holyhead. The *Meadowfield* was attacked on 9 July by German submarine UC-20 and sunk by gunfire off the south coast of Ireland while on a voyage from Huelva to Glasgow with a cargo of copper ore. One of the crew was killed and 28 survivors remained in an open boat for over seven hours before being rescued by a trawler and taken to Holyhead. U-boats would frequently sink ships by gunfire if this was possible; torpedoes would only be used for very large vessels because of their cost and the limited number of torpedoes that a submarine could carry.

The Defence of the Realm Act provided for many contingencies and one set of regulations concerned visible lighting. Lights were not meant to be visible to the enemy at sea. There followed a number of court cases where it was alleged that various individuals had breached these regulations. In July, a Mr James Ravenscroft of Harrison Drive, Rhosneigr, was charged with failing to obscure a light in one of the windows of his house. After some deliberation, the case was dismissed, but the bench 'hoped that Mr Ravenscroft would be very careful in future'. But William Jones of Red Wharf Bay was less lucky; he was found guilty of a similar offence and was fined 5s. The most absurd case to be reported was that of Thomas Lloyd of Ysgubor Lwyd, Gaerwen. Mr Lloyd was cycling from Llanfairfechan to Gaerwen late one evening, and claimed in court that he was aware of the lighting regulations. He cycled from Llanfairfechan without lights but at Abergwyngregyn he was instructed to light up. At Talybont, a policeman told him to extinguish his lights. In Bangor, he was told to light up, but at the 'look-out' in Upper Bangor he was told to extinguish them. In Llanfairpwll he was stopped by a policeman who told him to light up. This policeman noted his name and address. An exasperated Mr Lloyd said in court, 'I am willing to obey the Defence of the Realm Act, but I don't know what to do.' The policeman who stopped him at Llanfairpwll said in court, 'the order requiring lights to be extinguished does not apply to Llanfairpwll.' Mr Lloyd was fined 5s. According to the *Daily Despatch*, even David Lloyd George was stopped by a special constable who judged that his car lights were too bright. No action was taken against him.

On 4 August, it was announced that British losses in the first year of the war amounted to 76,000 killed, 252,000 wounded and 55,000 missing. On the same day, *Y Clorianydd* reported that 15,000 cigarettes had been sent to Holyhead Servicemen by Mr E.E. Huws, on behalf of a Holyhead amateur theatre company.

U-boats were continuing to make their presence felt in the Irish Sea. On 17 August 1915, two merchant vessels were torpedoed and sunk by U-38 not far from Bardsey Island (see Map 2 p. 32). They were the 3,596-ton *Paros* (built in 1898 and sailing from Karachi to Manchester with a cargo of wheat) and the 3,034-ton *Kirkby* (built in 1891 and sailing from Barry with a cargo of coal). The commander of the U-38 was Captain Max Valentiner (1883–1949). He achieved some notoriety during the war and was rated as the third highest scoring U-boat commander.

There was some concern at this time about water services at Holyhead. The Holyhead Water Company was forced to reduce the number of hours that water was available through the taps. The company stated that it intended to draw water from Llyn Traffwll but was unable to obtain suitable pumping equipment because suppliers were busy with the war effort.

Allied troops had landed in Gallipoli in April 1915 in an attempt to knock Turkey out of the war. Private R.R. Williams of Menai Bridge went missing on 12 August and the following paragraph appeared in *Y Clorianydd*:

MISSING – The worst is feared about Private R.R. Williams (19808), B. Co., 4th Battalion South Wales Borderers as he has been missing since the 12th of August after being in a battle in Gallipoli. If any other soldier knows anything about him, his parents at 9 Beach Road, Menai Bridge would very pleased to hear. Before joining the army, he worked at Port Sunlight soap works.
[Translated].

The worst fears of his parents must later have been realised. Private Richard Robert Williams is listed on the Menai Bridge War Memorial; he died on 10 August 1915, aged 19.

On 19 August, at a meeting of the Anglesey Enlistment Committee in Llangefni, it was decided to visit every man aged 18–40 who had not enlisted to ask him to explain why he had not done so. There was clearly some frustration that the recruitment process was not as rapid as the authorities would have wished; they were now bringing pressure to bear on individuals.

On 25 August 1915 the 15,801-ton *Arabic* (a passenger ship of the White Star Line) was sunk by German submarine U-24 with the loss of 48 lives. Only a few days later the 9,599-ton ocean liner *Hesperian* was sunk by U-20 off south-west Ireland on a voyage from Liverpool to Montreal with the loss of 32 lives. *Y Clorianydd* reported that a certain Mrs Jones of Ty'n y Pwll, Llanfaelog, was on board the *Hesperian*, but that she and the others on board had survived. Survivors from the *Hesperian* arrived in Holyhead on 9 September on the steamer *Rathmere* and were taken by train to Liverpool. A large crowd had gathered to see them; some were reported to be showing signs of injury. Both the *Hesperian* and *Arabic* incidents caused bitterness and disquiet in the United States of America. On 30 August, the Germans prohibited further action of this sort and American pressure was one of the factors behind their decision.

On 26 September 1915, the Llangefni Airship Station was commissioned and began its work. Initially there were four airships, known by the numbers SS18, SS24, SSW25 and SS32. These were used to patrol a large area extending from Anglesey to Dublin in the west and to Morecambe Bay in the east.

At the end of October, five women from Holyhead appeared before a Police Court (i.e. Magistrates Court) on charges which were described by *Y Clorianydd* as 'cerdded y strydoedd' (walking the streets). No further details were given. Two of them were fined £1 each or two weeks' imprisonment, and one of them was fined 10*s* or a week's imprisonment.

At the end of October, the *Chronicle* published another letter denouncing Nonconformist ministers for their apathy towards recruitment:

> North Wales has done less in supplying men for the army than any other part of Great Britain and I challenge contradiction, and this in a great measure is owing to the apathetic conduct of the chapel ministers in North Wales. . . . What do these so-called ministers or their flock care for the appeals made by the Government . . . so long as they can hold forth in their little 'Zion Chapel' drawing their pay, and unduly influencing their flock from doing their duty. . . . When will these persons put aside their milksop, sentimental resolutions, and be men. We don't want chaplains, we want soldiers. . . . This country has too long been chloroformed by these so-called Christian ministers, but public opinion will not forget when the war is over what part they took, and will set up a new religion. viz., the Gospel of Humanity. Yours, etc.

On 3 November *Y Clorianydd* published a letter from William Jones of Llannerch-y-medd who was serving in Gallipoli. The letter was written to his parents:

> . . . we are fighting hard day and night and hundreds of Turks are being killed here every day and also giving themselves up as prisoners. We are certain to win in the end. The Turks have women here who have been stationed in the woods in order to fire at us; they are nice-looking women and some of them are very young. . . . I have been lucky so far and I am grateful that I can tell you that John and myself are 'all right' and perfectly healthy. . . . I am only a hundred yards from John and I see him and Richard Francis every day and have a little chat with them now and again. The job I have is to guard the prisoners that we have captured – quite an easy, light job; so you see that I have not been a bad boy or I would not have been given such a job. Benjia Jones is with me, and we are contented here. From your dear son, William.
> [Translated]

The *Hibernian* came into service between Holyhead and Dublin as a passenger steamer for the London & North Western Railway Company in 1899. When the war began, the *Hibernian* was commandeered by the Admiralty, adapted as a patrol ship and renamed HMS *Tara*. In 1915, the *Tara* was sent to the eastern Mediterranean to patrol off the Egyptian coast. On Friday 5 November 1915 the German U-boat U-35 torpedoed the *Tara* as she made her way to Solum. The ship sank in 8 minutes and 33 seamen

(12 from Holyhead) were lost but 93 of the crew (including a number of Anglesey men) clambered into lifeboats and were towed by the submarine to Port Suliman as prisoners of war. They were put in the custody of the Turks. They were forced to march across rough terrain, deserts and mountains, and conditions were very grim. They slept in caves during the night. After many days of misery, exhaustion and lack of food, they were joined on 15 November by survivors of another boat, HMS *Moorina*, and the two groups of men remained together. Christmas and the New Year came and went with no sign of any change in their circumstances.

In a letter from the Revd John Williams of Brynsiencyn, published in *Y Clorianydd* in November 1915, it was explained that Brigadier-General Owen Thomas would be moving to the Kinmel Camp near Rhyl to command a new regiment. The military authorities had refused to allow Owen Thomas to lead his brigade into battle because of his age and lack of military experience. The Revd Williams wrote:

> A fortnight ago, it was understood that the War Office will not send out any General who is over 55 years of age. This was a bitter blow for him [Owen Thomas]. The same thing is true of chaplains but I believe that I shall receive special permission to visit France. [Translated]

The Revd Mr Williams was being optimistic; in fact, he was never allowed to go to France.

On 17 November 1915, the 1,862-ton hospital ship HMHS *Anglia* struck a mine laid by U-boat UC-5 in the Dover Strait. The *Anglia* sunk in less than 15 minutes a mile east of Folkestone. The *Anglia* had been built in 1900 and was used as an Irish Sea ferry until 1914. The ship was carrying 390 injured officers and servicemen together with doctors and nurses and the total number of people drowned was 134. The crew were mostly Anglesey men, 53 being from Holyhead and 21 of them died. It should be noted that different sources give varying numbers of casualties, but the loss to Anglesey was immense.

The Revd John Williams' mission to attract as many volunteers as possible was still in full swing. In November 1915, speaking in Welsh in the town square in Llangefni, he tried to shame the island's young men to enlist:

> You young rosy-cheeked lads of Anglesey, would you let pale-faced lads from the towns sacrifice their lives to keep you safe? Would you let your brothers cross the seas from America and Canada and Australia, while you live a carefree life at the periphery? The olive-skinned Indians can come in their thousands to fight for your freedom and your rights, while you bask in comfort and cosiness? Be men. Stand up fearlessly for your country, for your freedom and for your God. [Translated]

In the same month the Revd John Williams directed this plea towards the sons of prosperous farmers, few of whom had apparently volunteered:

Everyone makes sacrifices – banks, offices – and every [social] class. Young men earning large salaries are making sacrifices. Why have only seven farmers' sons joined the army? Come; I shall come with you.
[Translated]

Lieutenant Archibald Rees, son of the Revd J.A. Rees, Rector of Rhoscolyn, wrote to his father describing the conditions in the Dardanelles in late November. Despite the dreadful conditions, he seemed to be in good spirits:

Since I last wrote, I can safely say that I have been through the worst time of my life. On the night of 26 November, it started to rain early on. After about 2 hours' rain it was – well, to describe it better, one might say hell. It was not rain, but sheets of water from the sky. In no time the water in parts of the trenches was waist-deep and in no part was it under knee-deep. . . .

With the trenches full of men, you can imagine that the water soon became liquid mud. It was terrible. Well, to settle it all, for the whole of a night and morning we lived in a snow blizzard. That night and the two following nights we had very hard frosts. . . . The Turks had an even worse time of it than we did. According to a deserter, dozens of them drowned or died of exposure. They [the Turks] ran outside their trenches to try to keep themselves warm and to avoid the water and mud, so we 'potted' them off.

On 8 December an anonymous writer in *Y Clorianydd* gave his view on the state of recruitment in Anglesey:

The town [Holyhead] is under a cloud and many of its people are anxious and in mourning [because of the *Anglia* and *Tara* tragedies]. Holyhead understands the seriousness of the times and aware of the gravity of the war. Already there are over 1,500 Holyhead lads 'on active service'. There are nearly 1,500 in military age, the majority of them engaged in their duties at the railway station, the harbour and the sea.

There are a number of other parts of the county that have already done magnificently, Llannerch-y-medd, Menai Bridge, Amlwch and Llangefni. That is, I believe, the 'order of merit' of the towns. There is an honourable place also for Newborough, Dwyran and Brynsiencyn amongst the villages. As for the rest of the county, with the exception of a patch here and there and a few homes which have given to their country all they have, the less said the better, since the answer is far from satisfactory.
[Translated]

In December, the feeling of anger in Holyhead following the *Tara* and *Anglia* tragedies seemed to be boiling over into anti-German feeling. Much of this hatred was being directed at a certain Mr Scherzer, the Marine Catering Superintendent who was employed by the LNWR. Since he had a German, or German-sounding name, he was assumed to be of German parentage. This resentment was said to be very strong among railway company employees and in a letter, members of Holyhead Trades and Labour Council called on him to relinquish his position. Their letter ended: 'Failing a satisfactory reply within seven days, we shall be reluctantly compelled to resort to other measures.' In a footnote, the *Chronicle* stated that Mr Scherzer was British-born and the Home Office could take no action.

In the same month *Y Clorianydd* published a letter from an unnamed soldier in the Royal Welch Fusiliers serving on the front. He appears to be resigned to spending Christmas in the trenches:

. . . Despite the fact that I have barely three months' experience of the terrible war, it is quite enough to give an account. . . . If you were to ask me what sort of men the enemy are, I could not tell you, because I have not seen a single one of them. This is a strange battle – no one can see each other! The old German is exceptionally quiet at times, that that is the best way for him to be: if he raises the hackles of the old Welshman, he will regret it. It is clear that I shall spend Christmas this year in the 'dugout'. . . . I shall have to be satisfied with the delicious morsel known as 'bully beef' and a biscuit, that is, unless a Samaritan appears from somewhere. But I am perfectly happy and healthy. Warmest greetings, One from Llangristiolus.
[Translated]

In the final edition of the year, *Y Clorianydd* published a letter written by the Revd W. Llewelyn Lloyd of Llangaffo to W. Morris Williams, of Llangwyllog. The Revd W. Llewelyn Lloyd was a Presbyterian minister who was serving as a Chaplain on the Western Front:

. . . Please ask every church in which you preach to pray for us more sincerely than ever before. . . . I shall be selling coffee during the daytime this week and conducting meetings in the evening. . . . If you come across anyone who wishes to cheer up the Anglesey lads who are here, tell them to send cigarettes and cakes to me and I shall ensure that they receive them.
[Translated]

CHAPTER FOUR

1916

As the Revd John Williams explained in his letter to the press in November 1915, Brigadier-General Owen Thomas was persuaded to take command of a reserve brigade. He left Llandudno to take command at the Kinmel Camp, near Abergele on 15 January 1916.

Towards the end of January there was a call for the Home Office to print the 'Lighting Regulations' in Welsh in order to lessen the confusion that existed. The *Chronicle* stated, rather pompously, that it would be for 'the benefit of those who are not versed in the Saxon tongue.'

In the same month the *Chronicle* reported that the Anglesey Education Committee were being forced to make a 'rearrangement of staffs' since so many teachers had enlisted in the armed services. In the same issue it was reported that two teachers had been killed on active service. They were Private George A. Thomas (Cybi School, Holyhead) and Lance Corporal John Henry Jones (Llangefni Council School). Both men lived in Holyhead.

The initial rush to enlist voluntarily in the Army had reduced to a trickle by 1916 despite pressure being used against 'laggards' in an attempt to shame them into enlisting. In February, owing to the urgent need for men at the front, conscription was introduced for the first time in the war for single men and childless widowers aged 18–41. This was extended to all men, married or unmarried, on 25 May 1916. The National Service Act (1916) granted exemption to those in essential wartime employment, those who were medically unfit, religious ministers and also (for the first time) conscientious objectors. The Act remained in force until 1920 but conscription ceased when the war ended.

As the result of the introduction of conscription, a system of appeals tribunals was established to hear cases of men who believed they should be exempt from military service. These Military Tribunals were regularly held in all areas; they were kept very busy with large numbers claiming exemption. Details of these tribunals, including the names of those seeking exemption, were regularly reported in some detail in the local papers. Often, men would be granted exemption for a certain period, but would have to appear before the tribunal again at a later date. Sometimes employers would plead the case of one of their workers if it was felt their occupation was essential to their business. Conscientious objectors would also appear before tribunals to plead their case. The whole process was very public.

There were about 16,000 conscientious objectors throughout Britain during the course of the war and they were regarded by many as cowards and 'shirkers' and were vociferously condemned by letters in the local press. A Mr R. Jones Roberts left *Chronicle* readers in no doubt of his opinion:

The other day I had the doubtful pleasure of talking with several conscientious objectors on wars generally and this one in particular. Charles Kingsley said: 'We have to fight and kill, we want to be sure that God's blessing in our fighting and killing; we have to go into battle; and we want to know that there, too, we are doing God's work, and to be sure that God is on our side.' . . . No man was a greater lover of God and his neighbours than Charles Kingsley, whose words, I think, preclude the necessity for further comment. Yours, etc.,

Conscientious objectors were the target of this sarcastic letter which made reference to a captured German gun being exhibited in Holyhead:

Sir – One of the captured German guns will be exhibited in Holyhead this week, and its advent, however, will involve no risk to life or limb as the gun will be guarded by a special squad of conscientious objectors, whose presence will be sufficient guarantee of its absolute harmlessness. I thought the timid and the nervous of both sexes might like to be reassured on this point. Yours, etc., S. Bo.

On 21 February, the Siege of Verdun began; it was a major battle between French and German troops. Lasting until 18 December, it was the longest battle of the war and the bloodiest military engagement in history.

On 13 March, the Germans changed their policy regarding U-boats again. Now the submarines were allowed to sink British ships (except passenger ships) in home waters. However, American pressure caused this policy to be changed on 24 April; U-boats were then instructed not to sink vessels without warning.

On 17 March 1916, after 135 days in captivity, the survivors of the HMS *Tara* were unexpectedly rescued by a convoy of British vehicles led by the Duke of Westminster. The survivors were taken to Alexandria for treatment and recuperation before returning home as heroes. During April and May, the *Chronicle* reported the story in immense detail, and printed photographs of the survivors in Alexandria. A day-by-day account of their suffering in captivity was also described by a *Chronicle* reporter who travelled to Portsmouth to meet them as they returned home.

In early April, a scandal was slowly emerging at the Kinmel Camp which was under the command of Brigadier-General Owen Thomas. It seems that a lady by the name of Mary Adelaide Virginia Thomasina Eupatoria Cornwallis-West (the wife of Colonel William Cornwallis-West of Ruthin Castle) had formed a crush on a recovering soldier named Patrick Barrett. It is believed that Barrett was given a commission through her influence and she had bombarded him with amorous letters. Mrs Cornwallis-West (usually referred to 'Patsy') was a woman of strong character and an interesting and rather unorthodox history. She was said to have been a mistress of Prince of Wales (later King Edward VII) when she was only 16 years old. She must also have been quite eccentric as she was said to be very fond of sliding down stairs on a tray! Patrick Barrett's wife showed Brigadier-General Owen Thomas the letters written to her husband by Mrs Cornwallis-West and Owen Thomas passed the matter to his superiors.

In the early part of the year, it was reported that all the Belgian refugees had left Menai Bridge as they had found work in England. All the furniture and household effects in the houses they occupied in Nant Terrace (Cadnant Road) were to be sold. The Belgian Promenade, which they helped to build, is still a lasting reminder of their time in the town.

On Easter Monday, 24 April 1916, Irish Republicans rose against the British and seized key points in Dublin. The 'Easter Rebellion', as it is often called, was crushed within five days but 450 people were killed, including 116 British servicemen. For a government actively pursuing a war in Europe and elsewhere, this proved to be an additional and unwanted headache. At the beginning of May, it was reported that 489 Sinn Féin prisoners, all men, had arrived from Ireland in Holyhead, presumably on their way to prisons in England. The *Chronicle* described them as a 'motley crowd'.

Menai Bridge's Belgian promenade was completed in early 1916.

At the beginning of May, the *Chronicle* reported an 'unusual sight' at Wern Farm, Llangoed. Due to the scarcity of agricultural labourers, farmer's daughter Miss Madge Hughes and the maidservant were harrowing and rolling, and 'took to their new occupation with pride and some skill'. Their action elicited 'warm commendation' from a military representative at a local military tribunal, in the hope that other Anglesey farmers would follow the 'timely and worthy example' of the Hughes family.

At midnight on 7 May, the 183-ton three-masted wooden schooner *James W. Fisher* was wrecked close to the shore off Bull Bay (see Map 2, p. 32). The vessel was carrying coal from Ellesmere Port to Granville. One of the crew (described by the *Chronicle* as a 'dishevelled foreigner') swam ashore and alerted local residents, but the other five members of the crew could not be found and were presumed to have drowned. The incident was not believed to have been the result of enemy action.

On 13 May, a 46-year-old John Elias, a watch and clock repairer, was shot dead at Llanfaethlu. Police were alerted by his father, also named John Elias, and they discovered his body with a gun beside him. A few days later, John Elias Snr was charged with his murder after the police had decided that the son's injuries could not have been self-inflicted. The case was heard at Anglesey Assizes in Beaumaris on 3 June amid great excitement. The newspapers reported the trial in great detail. John Elias Snr was found guilty of his son's murder and was sentenced to death. The legal process in 1916 was very swift and very brutal – from crime to gallows in three weeks.

In May 1916 the British coaster *Saxon* which had been seized in Hamburg by the Germans in August 1914 was requisitioned by the Imperial German Navy.

On 5 June, Lord Kitchener, the Minister for War, was drowned when HMS *Hampshire*, taking him to Russia on war business (accompanied by his personal staff and officials from the Foreign Office and the Ministry of Munitions), was sunk by a mine off Orkney. Following his death, David Lloyd George became Secretary of State for War.

On 21 June, Brigadier-General Owen Thomas was suddenly and unexpectedly relieved of his position at the Kinmel Camp. Owen Thomas' departure was shrouded in some mystery, and this matter, as well as the earlier Mrs Cornwallis-West affair, would together cause something of a crisis in the War Office leading to an enquiry. Owen Thomas' successor at Kinmel, Colonel Cuthbertson, began his duties on 28 June.

The First Battle of the Somme between British and French forces and German troops began in France on 1 July 1916. There were 57,470 British casualties on the first day alone; over 19,000 were killed. The battle lasted until 18 November 1916.

The war was now reported to be costing £6,000,000 a day. In order to further fund the war effort, War Savings Certificates were introduced. They were purchased at 15*s* 6*d* each and the government undertook to repay £1 after five years.

During 1916 it was clear that some men were not presenting themselves before military tribunals after being summoned to do so. The *Chronicle* printed a lengthy list of those men who had failed to turn up and the public was asked to provide information as to their whereabouts to the local Recruiting Officers.

In Holyhead, there were reports that a tall, masked man had carried out a number of burglaries in the town. Some householders had been startled by this intruder and considerable anxiety had been caused. The matter remained a mystery; the newspapers made no further mention of the masked man in subsequent editions.

On 11 August, two vessels, the *Skernahan* and the *Yorkshire*, were involved in a collision 8 miles west of South Stack. The crews were saved and brought ashore. Also, on the same day, the schooner *King's Hill* sank after being involved in a collision with an unknown ship 6 miles from Caernarfon Bay Light Ship. Fortunately the crew survived.

On 1 September, a man called Conrad Greenberg appeared in court charged under the Defence of the Realm Act with being a 'suspected person'. He had been seen loitering in Holyhead railway station in the evening, under the influence of drink. He proclaimed, 'I am a Russian, but I stick up for England.' A policeman stated Mr Greenberg's papers were in order and so the case was dismissed.

In October 1916, the Welsh-language anti-war monthly *Y Deyrnas* [The Realm] was published for the first time in Bangor. It was edited by Thomas Rees, Principal of Bala-Bangor Theological College and an uncompromising pacifist. Also associated with *Y Deyrnas* was blind Presbyterian minister John Puleston Jones, another fervent opponent of the war. *Y Deyrnas* achieved a circulation figure of about 3,000 copies, but was never particularly influential and sales in Anglesey were said to be low.

On a stormy night on 3 November, the steamship *Connemara* sank at the entrance to Carlingford Lough in Ireland after being struck by the coal ship *Retriever*. The *Connemara* sank within minutes. The 30 crew members (all from Anglesey, notably Holyhead and Amlwch) and the 51 passengers on the *Connemara*, as well as 8 crew members from the *Retriever* died. Only one person survived the tragedy – one of the crew members from the *Retriever*. A fund was established to help the bereaved and by January 1917 over £1,460 had been collected. Just a day after the sinking in Ireland, the 4,278-ton *Skerries* was mined and sunk about half way between the Isle of Man and Point Lynas (see Map 2, p. 32). Two lives were lost.

In mid-November the *Chronicle* revealed details of a Christmas Pudding Fund, run in conjunction with the *Daily Telegraph*. The intention was to send Christmas puddings to soldiers at the front. Sixpence would buy one pudding.

At the end of November it was announced that Hugh Pritchard of Llangefni had relinquished his commission with the Royal Welsh Fusiliers and was engaged with the work of organising the Volunteer Movement in Anglesey. It was hoped that a county battalion could be formed. It was proposed to form detachments in all the towns as well as in each village. Six hundred men would be needed for the War Office to recognise them as a battalion and the scheme was open to anyone of 17 years of age or over and physically fit.

In December it was announced that men who presented themselves at tribunals and were found to be medically unfit twice would receive discharge certificates and would not be called to any further tribunals. It became commonplace, however, that if men were exempted from military service, it would be conditional on their joining the Volunteer Movement.

In mid-December, John Sullivan, a private in the Australian Imperial Forces, was travelling by train from Holyhead. Apparently he felt unwell when the train was near the Bodorgan tunnels, and he opened the train window to vomit. As he did so, he struck his head and was seriously injured. He died in hospital at Bangor.

It was revealed in December that a report was awaited concerning the circumstances of Owen Thomas' departure from the Kinmel Camp earlier in the year. Owen Thomas himself was quoted as saying, 'The report is satisfactory to me.' A few days before Christmas, Ian McPherson (Under Secretary for War) made a statement to the House of Commons:

> . . . action that was taken in his [Owen Thomas] case was due entirely to military requirements and not to any undue influence . . . would take this opportunity of thanking the gallant officer for the great services he has rendered in recruiting for Welsh regiments. With regard to the lady implicated in the case, she is outside the jurisdiction of the military control.

CHAPTER FIVE

1917

In January, further information came to light concerning Brigadier-General Owen Thomas. The *Chronicle* reported (under the heading 'Army Scandal') that on 25 September 1915 (while he was still at Llandudno) an internal army report maintained that Brigadier-General Owen Thomas was lacking in military knowledge and training, and he was recommended for command of a reserve brigade. He was persuaded to accept command of the 14th (Reserve) Infantry Brigade which he did on 15 January 1916. On 10 May in the same year, a certain Lieutenant-General Sir Pitcairn Campbell reported that Owen Thomas was 'one who was considered should be replaced as opportunities offered.' This constituted an adverse report concerning Owen Thomas' fitness for his command and this was apparently not made known to him at the time. Shortly after Lord Kitchener's death on 5 June, things seemed to change and Owen Thomas was relieved of his duties on 21 June 1916. These details also make reference to Mrs Cornwallis-West, described by the press as a woman 'of irrepressible beauty and charm'. There was a suggestion that she, and possibly her husband, had been meddling in army matters that did not concern them. It is thought that Mrs Cornwallis-West had written to Sir John Cowans (the Quartermaster-General of the Army) asking that some fault be found with Owen Thomas so that he could be relieved of his command and be replaced by T.A. Wynne-Edwards, Deputy Lieutenant of Denbighshire, and a friend of the Cornwallis-West family. This case was closely followed by the *Chronicle* and *Y Clorianydd*, both keen to report local interest in Owen Thomas. But the affair was also a massive government scandal which the national press reported in detail.

The treatment meted out to Owen Thomas caused considerable protest. Anglesey County Council, among others, called on the government, in the national interest, to publish the full report of the Court of Inquiry and the minutes of the evidence upon which the report was based.

In January 1917, the government announced the establishment of a new voluntary service, the Women's Auxiliary Army Corps (WAAC) and it was officially started on 28 March. In Anglesey, the Revd John Williams encouraged young women to join the armed forces but he was heavily criticised for doing so.

At the end of January, Rhosneigr railway station was closed by the LNWR as a temporary wartime economy measure. The station had been opened in 1907 to cater for the tourist trade then beginning to flourish in the area. It was the last Anglesey station to be built on the main Chester to Holyhead line.

On 1 February, Germany declared unrestricted submarine warfare for the third time. Two days later, the United States severed diplomatic relations with Germany. By this time, the Germans felt that they could disregard any American objections as US involvement in the war was imminent. Of all Allied and neutral ships sunk by U-boat action during the war, 72 per cent were lost in 1917 and 1918 alone. By 1917, the movement of U-boats in the English Channel was severely restricted by a barrage in the Dover Strait and this resulted in increased activity in the Irish Sea, the area patrolled by the Llangefni Airship Station and the Holyhead Naval Base. In 1917, about 14 ships were lost around Anglesey and the Bardsey Island area which was patrolled by the Llangefni Airship Station. There was significant loss of life.

On 10 February, the 325-ton *Sallagh* was sunk off Bardsey Island with the loss of one life (see Map 2, p. 32). The following day the 242-ton *Olivia* was sunk in the same area by UC-65 with the loss of one life. On 14 February, UC-65 also torpedoed and sank three ships in the Bardsey Island area: the 791-ton *Ferga*, the 375-ton *Margarita* and the 1,763-ton *Greenland*. No lives were lost. On the following day, the 564-ton *Kyanite* was sunk in the same area by UC-65, without loss of life. Some of the crews who survived these attacks were brought to Holyhead and sent home by rail.

In a Commons question on 16 February, the Prime Minister was asked to publish the full report of the Owen Thomas scandal. Mr Ian McPherson replied that it would not be in the national interest to do so, even though just a few days earlier, Owen Thomas had received a knighthood in the Honours List. On 20 February, Mr Ian McPherson made a further statement in the Commons:

> . . . [Owen Thomas] was removed from his command under circumstances which involved no reflection whatever upon him. . . .The removal must be regarded as having taken place owing to his not being suitable for the special work which brigades were expected to do, and not for any inefficiency in the services he had rendered, and particularly in his services towards recruiting.

In 1917, powers under the Defence of the Realm Act were used by the government to take over 2.5 million acres of land for farming. Help with the additional agricultural work was provided by the Women's Land Army (set up by the government's Food Production Department) and by conscientious objectors. Initially, women in the Land Army were paid about £1 2s 6d for a typical 50-hour week. The harvest failed in 1917 and at one point Britain was left with only three weeks' reserve of food so that famine became a distinct possibility. To make matters worse, horses (then the main motive power on most farms) were hard to find as so many had been commandeered by the forces and taken to the front.

On 1 March, at a well-attended event in the Pier Pavilion at Llandudno, Sir Owen Thomas was presented with a silver cigarette case and a badge in the form of a leek by the Honourable Mrs Lloyd Mostyn. A few days later, Sir Owen Thomas visited his old home at Neuadd, Cemaes. He was reported to have commented, 'The recent inquiry was a harder fight than in the trenches.'

On 2 March, Miss Davies, of the prominent Treborth family, opened a new club for girls in Holyhead – the Girls' Patriotic Club. The club leader, a Miss Howe, claimed that 135 girls had already joined and she promised 'wholesome recreation of all kinds'.

On 21 March, the 1988-ton Norwegian cargo ship *Svendsholm* was torpedoed and sunk by German submarine U-24 south-west of Ireland while en route from Londonderry to St Thomas and thankfully there were no casualties. An Anglesey man, Captain William John Hughes of Brynsiencyn, was one of those responsible for rescuing a number of crew members from the *Svendsholm*.

On 24 March the 592-ton *Fairearn*, on a voyage from Garston to Cork with coal, was captured by U-65 16 miles north-west of South Stack (see Map 2, p. 32). Four days later, the 4,662-ton *Snowdon Range* was torpedoed and sunk without warning 25 miles west of Bardsey, with the loss of four lives. The crew were in boats for nearly ten hours before being picked up by the *Somerset Court* off South Stack and being landed in Holyhead. The following day, the British steamer *Crispin* was torpedoed and sunk by U-57 off the south-east coast of Ireland and some of those who survived were landed at Holyhead.

At the end of March, the government announced that no petrol was to be provided for private motoring. Only essential use by certain people would qualify for fuel. In a county with very few private cars, this would not have affected the ordinary folk of Anglesey to any great degree.

Because of the food shortage, a number of schools on the island decided to introduce gardening. In April 1917, the log book of Llanddaniel Fab primary school noted: 'Gardening introduced to the school, part of the boys' playground taken over for such purpose. Planted potatoes, broad and French beans.'

On 6 April, the United States of America declared war on Germany and the first American troops reached France on 26 June 1917.

On 20 April, the *Chronicle* published a front page announcement from the National Free Church Council of Wales calling for 'the prohibition of the manufacture and sale of intoxicating liquors during the war and for six months afterwards.' The advertisement claimed that the manufacture of beer had a damaging effect on the supply of sugar and bread.

In May there was a serious paper shortage and some weeks the *Chronicle* was reduced from its usual eight pages to only four. There had already been an increase in its price, from 1*d* at the beginning of the war, to 1½*d* in December 1916 and to 2*d* in February 1917.

In June 1917, the airships at the Royal Naval Air Service station near Llangefni were replaced by others of updated design, known as SSP1, SSP5 and SSP6.

Also in June, an assembly known as the Irish Convention was set up by David Lloyd George. It sat between July 1917 and March 1918 to address the question of

Irish Home Rule. The Government of Ireland Act had been passed in May 1914, but progress in finding a permanent solution had inevitably been delayed by the war.

The Welsh poet Ellis Humphrey Evans of Trawsfynydd (known by his bardic name Hedd Wyn) died on the Pilckem ridge during the first day of the Battle of Passchendaele on 31 July 1917 at the age of 30. Unbeknown to him he had won the chair at the Welsh National Eisteddfod held that year in Birkenhead. Hedd Wyn became known as Bardd y Gadair Ddu (The Bard of the Black Chair) and is still remembered today as one of the many young people whose lives were needlessly cut short in the appalling trenches of the battlefield. On the same day on which Hedd Wyn died, 31,000 other soldiers were killed in the same battle.

On 10 July, a fire destroyed a house near Menai Bridge. Cartrefle was described as a 'charming residence on the banks of the Menai Straits', owned by Mr and Mrs Fred Turner. Two maids observed smoke and alerted the Menai Bridge Fire Brigade who attended the scene with their 'new steam fire engine'. The Bangor fire engine also attended and pumped sea water with the assistance of wounded soldiers from Bodlondeb Red Cross Hospital at Treborth.

On 17 July 1917, King George V decreed that the royal family's surname be changed from the Germanic-sounding Saxe-Coburg-Gotha to Windsor. At the same time the closely related Battenberg family changed their name to Mountbatten.

On the same day, an incident at sea would result in the award of the Victoria Cross to an Amlwch man who was serving on a Q-ship. The Q-ships were an Allied response to the ever-present threat posed by German U-boats, especially in the latter part of the war. Essentially, the Q-ships were old coastal vessels, often at the end of their useful lives, which had been specially adapted and heavily armed to act as decoy vessels for German U-boats. By the end of the war, there were 366 such ships in service. In the event of an attack by a U-boat, the crew of the Q-ship followed a standard procedure of lowering a lifeboat in order to give the impression that the crew were going to abandon ship. The Q-ship's formidable arsenal of guns was hidden and the camouflage would only be removed after the U-boat surfaced. The Q-ship's guns would then open fire and hopefully sink the submarine.

On 17 July, the 2,800-ton Q-ship *Pargust* was off the coast of Ireland when she was torpedoed by the coastal mine-layer UC-29. The usual procedure was followed, but the torpedo had damaged part of the camouflage and if it were to fall, the guns would be revealed. One of those on board the *Pargust*, 26-year-old William Williams (of the Royal Naval Reserve) from Amlwch,

William Williams, originally from Amlwch, was awarded the VC,DSM and Bar and the French Médaille Militaire in 1917.

supported the entire weight of the camouflage on his shoulders for over half an hour while waiting for the U-boat to surface. When it appeared, the camouflage was released and the submarine was sunk by gunfire after a few minutes. Only two of the U-boat's crew survived.

The military authorities decided to award the Victoria Cross, but were unsure to whom it should be awarded. However, following a ballot among the ratings on the *Pargust*, William Williams was elected to receive the VC in the name of the whole crew. This was his second award; he had been awarded the Distinguished Service Medal (DSM) for his part in the sinking of German submarine U-83 on 17 February 1917 by the Q-ship *Farnborough*. Furthermore, just three weeks after the *Pargust* incident, on 8 August, William Williams was awarded a bar to his DSM (in other words a second award) for his part in the sinking of a German submarine off the French coast by the *Dunraven*. He therefore earned three gallantry awards in six months. In addition, he was also awarded the French Médaille Militaire. William Williams is believed to be the most decorated serviceman of the First World War.

On 31 July the Third Battle of Ypres began (near the Belgian village of Passchendaele). The battle, between Allied and German troops, lasted until 6 November and the great number of casualties caused considerable damage to the morale of British troops.

During the war, more land was brought into cultivation and this had resulted in a considerable financial return for farmers. Anglesey's farmers were no exception; many had reaped the benefit of high prices for meat, milk and bread. But working class families had enjoyed no such prosperity. They were forced to pay higher prices for essentials while earning a low wage. In rural communities such as Anglesey, farm workers became hostile towards the farmers whom they saw as profiteering at their expense. The farmers were widely condemned; furthermore their use of child labour fuelled further unrest. *Y Clorianydd* published five articles by W.J. Jones of Brynsiencyn (also known as Brynfab) between July and September 1917, drawing the attention of its readers to the pitiful conditions in which many rural people lived and the excessive profits made by farmers.

The Corn Production Bill of 1917 gave farmers minimum prices if they ploughed grassland to grow more corn. Furthermore agricultural workers were to be guaranteed a minimum wage, to be fixed by a Wages Board and agreed locally.

Undeb Gweithwyr Môn (Anglesey Workers' Union) had been formed in 1909 as a local union to safeguard the working conditions of Anglesey workers, primarily though not exclusively, farm labourers. *Undeb Gweithwyr Môn* launched an intensive membership campaign in 1917–18 and this proved successful.

In late August Owen Jones of Tan'rallt, Llangristiolus, was charged with 'negligently failing to cultivate a field', described as being part of Carrog Farm, for oats or other grain in accordance with the requirements of a notice served upon him by the Executive Committee of the Anglesey War Agricultural Committee. This case was the first of its kind on the island. The penalty was surprisingly lenient – only £5.

In a Holyhead court in late August, Private George Williams, 13 Rhosgaer Avenue, Holyhead, was charged with being a deserter from the Royal Welch Fusiliers since 2 March 1917. He was remanded in custody to await a response from the Army. His parents were charged with aiding and abetting and were each sentenced to one month's imprisonment. This case was the first such case in Holyhead; one of the magistrates stated that the parents' punishment was 'lenient'. Considering the dreadful conditions in the trenches and the appalling loss of life, perhaps it is hardly surprising that men deserted.

Edward Jones (1883–1945), originally from Llangoed, was a gunner in Gibraltar where he was stationed from 1917 to 1919. His wife and four sons were living in Tregarth, near Bangor at the time. Servicemen stationed in Gibraltar were fortunate to be in a comparatively safe place, but this did not lessen the 'hiraeth' they felt for their homeland and their families. Writing in the Welsh Wesleyan Methodist denominational weekly Y Gwyliedydd Newydd (The New Sentinel) on 7 August 1917 he describes what he observed on a Sunday night in July in Main Street, Gibraltar. This would have struck an uncomfortable note with many and readers of this religious weekly (as well as most of the people of Anglesey) would have found it profoundly disturbing:

> . . . we shall never forget what we saw. Such drunkenness and filthy behaviour, the fighting and the shouting, the swearing and the cursing, and all this on a Sunday night. . . . Nothing was too base and unclean for them to commit. . . . There are a number of men who arrived here at the same time as me, in December 1916, who are now slaves to their lust; those who were previously excellent men have failed to resist the temptations of the army.
> [Translated].

In another letter in the same weekly on 18 September 1917, Edward Jones describes how he heard about his father's death and the pain this caused him:

> On the 13th of August, I received a letter from home informing me of my father's death. This was a terribly hard blow for me. He had been sick for some time and had been confined to his bed since Whitsun. In spite of being warned to expect the worst, it was a heavy blow and I shall never forget that dark, obscure day when I had to believe that his spirit had flown to his maker. Neither shall I forget the last time I saw him, on 26 October 1916. I went home to say goodbye. I shall always remember how we shook hands that day. I can still see the tear glistening in his eye. He spoke very little, but I could understand the language of his heart. He followed me to the door and remained there until I had disappeared from view. . . . One of the first things I shall do, if the Lord permits me to return home, is to visit that sacred spot where he lies.
> [Translated].

About this time there was an almost daily spate of Russians of military age arriving in Holyhead with the intention of travelling to Ireland by ferry. Such persons were routinely questioned by the authorities at Holyhead where an Aliens' Officer was permanently stationed. Many of these Russians claimed to be British or Irish and their intention was to evade military service. Typically they were sentenced to prison terms.

On 13 October, the 2,293-ton *Eskmere* was sunk by UC-75 about 15 miles north-west of South Stack while en route from Belfast to Barry (see Map 2, p. 32). Twenty lives were lost.

In November 1917, six Airco DH4 aircraft were to be brought into service at Llangefni Airship Base in order to assist the work of patrolling the Irish Sea on account of the large increase in U-boat activity in the area. The six aircraft left an airbase in London on 7 November, but encountered bad weather as they reached North Wales. Four of the aircraft decided to land at an airfield near Queensferry, but the remaining two decided to continue their journey to Anglesey. Due to continuing bad weather, the pilot of one of them decided to land on the Lafan Sands, near Abergwyngregyn. The plane landed successfully without loss of life, but the aircraft could not be recovered intact. The remaining aircraft continued its journey towards Anglesey and, as it approached the base, it crashed, killing the pilot Lieutenant Barnard Robert Hadon Carter (aged 19), the son of a Gloucester cleric. His passenger, Corporal Harold Smith, was badly injured. An inquest was told that the pilot turned his aircraft too sharply in a gusty wind and lost control. This was the first fatal aircraft accident in Anglesey.

After over three years of conflict with unprecedented casualties, the nation was weary of the war. So, too, were the servicemen, some of whom had not seen their families for years. Edward Jones, writing in *Y Gwyliedydd Newydd* on 20 November 1917, stated:

We hope that before this time next year the sword shall be in its scabbard, the cannon shall be silent and the weapons of destruction shall have ceased to spit death and that peace shall reign in the world, and that we, as children of captivity, shall experience peace as in days gone by.
[Translated]

Few would have disagreed with him.

Conscientious objectors were comparatively few in relation to the total number who entered war service. A conscientious objector would find himself brought before a military tribunal where he could expect to be aggressively questioned. Pressure would be brought to bear for him to accept other work in connection with the war. It was not unknown for conscientious objectors to be given dangerous work as stretcher-bearers on the front line as 'punishment' for their stance. Some conscientious objectors refused to accept any work related to the war. One such objector was the Revd Ben Meyrick of Penysarn, near Amlwch, a Baptist Minister who was ordained in May 1917. In October 1917, he was tried and sentenced to two years' hard labour for refusing to perform war work of any kind, in other words refusing to accept any 'alternative service'. He had previously been summoned to appear before Bangor magistrates (on 3 July) and had been fined £2 and escorted under military guard to a camp in Wrexham. According to the anti-war monthly *Y Deyrnas* (*The Realm*), this was the first occasion where the authorities had withheld the right of an ordained minister of religion not to enlist in the army. He was later held at Litherland awaiting his trial. There was little public sympathy for such people. In fact, Anglesey's local papers made no mention of this case. The Wesleyan weekly paper, *Y Gwyliedydd Newydd*, published an 'open letter to a conscientious objector'; curiously, it made no reference to Ben Meyrick by name, but was almost certainly inspired by his case.

On 24 November a Red Cross Sale for the parishes of Penmynydd, Llanedwen and Llanfair Pwllgwyngyll was held at the Council School, Llanfair Pwllgwyngyll. The Marquess of Anglesey was unable to be present on account of military commitments and the sale was opened by the Honourable Mrs Stapleton-Cotton. Such events were commonplace throughout Anglesey and they made a significant contribution to the work of organisations such as the Red Cross.

On 28 November 1917, the 7,832-ton merchant ship *Apapa* was sunk while on a voyage from Lagos to Liverpool with passengers and general cargo. A total of 77 lives were lost, 40 of them passengers. There were 64 survivors, who were taken to hospital at Holyhead. The *Apapa* was a comparatively new ship (built in 1914), which was defensively armed. She was torpedoed without warning by German U-boat U-96. The *Apapa* was torpedoed on her starboard side towards the stern. This occurred near the tiny island of Middle Mouse off the north coast of Anglesey (see Map 2, p. 32). As the passengers and crew were being transferred to the lifeboats, a second torpedo struck, swamping some of the lifeboats and causing the ship's funnel to collapse on to a lifeboat which was ready to be lowered into the water. It was this second torpedo that caused the majority of the casualties. In *The Times* of 10 December one of the survivors described the discharge of the second torpedo as 'cold-blooded murder' as it prevented many from being saved off the stricken ship.

On 30 November 1917, the 3,161-ton *Derbent* was sunk by U-96 about 6 miles north-east of Point Lynas with its cargo of fuel oil (see Map 2, p. 32). No lives were lost. The *Derbent* was owned by the Admiralty and was on a voyage from Liverpool to Queenstown (Cóbh).

In December advertisements started appearing in the local press for gas bags to run cars and other vehicles on coal gas (i.e. ordinary household gas) as an alternative to petrol. The gas bag would be secured to the roof of the vehicle. Various patriotic reasons were offered for undergoing this conversion, such as less petrol, more explosives, etc.

On 7 December, the 4,448-ton *Earl of Elgin* was torpedoed and sunk by UC-75 about 10 miles south-west of Caernarfon Bay light vessel (see Map 2, p. 32). Eighteen lives were lost. On 19 December the 2,898-ton *Clwyd* sank after a collision with another steamer 12 miles north of the Skerries. The *Clwyd*, owned by the Point of Ayr Colliery, was on a voyage from Dublin to Point of Ayr. The collision occurred in darkness and the other steamer was not seen by the seven crew members of the *Clwyd* who took to the boats and drifted for 34 hours without food or water. Eventually they were picked up by the trawler *Fly* of Fleetwood and taken to Douglas. The chief engineer of the *Clwyd*, William Owen Jones died of exposure. An inquiry held on 12 March 1918 ruled that the Dublin steamship *Paragon* was responsible for the collision. Collisions of this type were commonplace since ships were not lit at night owing to the threat from U-boats.

On Christmas Day the 3,463-ton ocean liner *Agberi* was torpedoed and sunk by U-87 about 18 miles north-west of Bardsey while on a voyage from Dakar to Liverpool. Those on board were rescued by one of its escorting vessels and there were no casualties. The U-boat was sunk by another escorting vessel. Two days later the 685-ton *Adela* was torpedoed and sunk 12 miles north-west of the Skerries with the loss of 24 lives.

CHAPTER SIX

1918

By 1918 there were 23,000 members of the Women's Land Army working on British farms. Of course, there were also many more women working on the land who were not part of the Land Army. In Anglesey, there were a total of over 2,000 women working on the land.

As a result of the German U-boat campaign against British and Allied merchant ships and despite the efforts of the Agricultural Committees and the Land Army, food was beginning to become scarce. As a result, food rationing was progressively introduced, and over the first few months of 1918, a number of basic foods were rationed, such as sugar, tea, margarine, bacon, cheese, butter and meat.

On 18 January, the late Captain John Fox-Russell of Holyhead was posthumously awarded the Victoria Cross. Captain Fox-Russell was a qualified doctor, born in Holyhead in 1893 and was serving with the Royal Army Medical Corps. He had previously been awarded the Military Cross. He married in 1916 but was killed in action in Palestine on 6 November 1917 and buried near Beersheba. The official citation stated:

> For most conspicuous bravery displayed in action – until he was killed Captain Russell repeatedly went out to attend the wounded under murderous fire from snipers and machine guns, and in many cases, when no other means were at hand, carried them himself although almost exhausted. He showed the greatest possible degree of valour.

Shipping Losses Escalate

German submarines continued to cause havoc in the seas patrolled by the Llangefni Airship Station and the Holyhead Naval Base with an even greater loss of life. In fact, the first three months of 1918 saw very severe losses at sea. On 26 January, the 1,232-ton *Cork* came under torpedo fire from U-103 and sank 9 miles north-east of Amlwch. Seven passengers and five of the crew died. Three days later the 3,257-ton *Ethelinda* was torpedoed and sunk 15 miles north-west of the Skerries with the loss of 26 lives. On 4 February, the 4,160-ton *Treveal* was sunk 10 miles north of the

Skerries after being torpedoed without warning by a German U-boat (see Map 2, p. 32). Thirty-three lives were lost, including the captain. The following day U-101 sunk the 5,078-ton *Mexico City* 15 miles south-west of South Stack, with the loss of 29 lives. Survivors were picked up by the *Leinster* and landed at Holyhead.

On 8 February, the *Chronicle* published 'a stirring account of heroic deeds by Welsh troops', relating the events of the great battles at Pilckem and Mametz Wood. In the same issue it was reported that the Welsh Heroes' Memorial fund stood at £61,000.

On 20 February the 1,527-ton *Djerv* was torpedoed and sunk 12 miles north-west of the Skerries with the loss of two lives (see Map 2, p. 32). Three days later, the 3,287-ton *British Viscount* was sunk 12 miles north-west of the Skerries, while en route from Liverpool to the Irish port of Queenstown (now known as Cóbh). Six lives were lost. Just days later on 23 February the 5,873-ton Royal Fleet Auxiliary tanker *Birchleaf* was torpedoed and shelled 20 miles north-west of the Skerries by U-91. The ship, which was built in 1916, was travelling between Devonport and Liverpool and the vessel suffered extensive damage though remained afloat. Two of the crew of 42 were killed. The survivors who landed at Holyhead related how the Germans took the captain of the *Birchleaf* prisoner on board the U-boat. Ships of the Holyhead Flotilla, including the American destroyer *Burrows*, immediately searched for U-91 and dropped depth charges, possibly unaware at that point that the *Birchleaf*'s skipper was on board. Consequently, it was believed that U-91 may have been damaged or destroyed. So what was the fate of the captain?

In fact, U-91 was undamaged and went on to sink many other ships throughout 1918 before surrendering in November. Further research reveals that the captain of the *Birchleaf* ended up in an internment camp for officers in a castle at Beeskow in Germany (45 miles south-east of Berlin), where he remained until the end of the war. His name was Ellis Morris Roberts (aged 47) of Glanrafon House, Llangoed. The *Birchleaf* underwent repairs and re-entered service in May 1918. After the war, the ship was renamed *British Birch* and she was eventually broken up in Glasgow in 1932.

On 27 February, St Maelog's Church, Llanfaelog, held a service to celebrate the purchase of its new 310-pipe organ. The organ had been purchased through the fundraising efforts of parishioners who had held garden fetes and other events throughout the previous summer. As a rural church, St Maelog's considered itself fortunate to have acquired an organ of such quality.

Attacks by U-boats continued apace and losses during March in the area patrolled by Llangefni Airship Station and Holyhead Naval Base were considerable. They form a depressing catalogue of lost ships and many deaths. On 1 March the 3,710-ton *Penvearn* was torpedoed and sunk 15 miles north-west of South Stack with the loss of 21 lives (see Map 2, p. 32). The following day, the 3,583-ton *Carmelite*, en route from Bilbao to Cardiff with a cargo of iron ore, was torpedoed without warning and sunk by U-105 about 10 miles south-west of the Calf of Man with the loss of two lives. On the same day the 1,330-ton *Kenmare* was torpedoed and sunk 25 miles north-west of the Skerries with the loss of 29 lives. On 3 March, the *Romeo* was sunk near the Skerries by U-102; it is believed that only three of the crew of 37 survived. One of them was landed at Holyhead by the patrol boat *Kilgobnet*. On 7 March, the 3,018-ton *Tarbetness* was torpedoed and sunk 12 miles south-west of the Caernarfon Bay light vessel. No lives were lost. The following day, the 167-ton *Erica* was sunk by U-110 5 miles south-west of Bardsey. The survivors landed on the Anglesey coast in their own boat. On 12 March, the 2,828-ton Spanish steamer *Arno Mendi* was torpedoed by UC-75 while en route from Agua Amarga to Ayr with a cargo of copper ore. The wreck lies 12 miles north-west of the Skerries. Of the crew of 25, only nine survived and they arrived ashore on life rafts. On 17 March, the 157-ton *Cressida* was sunk 16 miles north-west of the Skerries, with the loss of three lives. On the same day, the 976-ton *Sea Gull* was sunk 7 miles north-east of Point Lynas with the loss of at least 20 lives. On 23 March, the 4,241-ton *Anteros* was torpedoed and sunk 16 miles north-west of South Stack with the loss of two lives. On 30 March, the 1,166-ton *Slieve Bloom*, owned by the LNWR, sank after being in collision 4 miles north-west of South Stack with the American warship USS *Stockton*. No lives were lost.

On 6 March 1918 the British submarine H5 was sunk off Anglesey (about 15 miles south-west of Aberffraw) after being in collision with a vessel later identified as the *Rutherglen*. All those on board the H5 were killed, including an American naval officer. It seems the *Rutherglen* rammed the H5 believing it to be a U-boat. The *Rutherglen* later docked at Holyhead and reported sinking a U-boat. However, the H5 was missing and the truth soon became apparent. A plaque commemorating the 26 who died on the H5 was dedicated on the Armed Forces Day at Holyhead in 2010. The H5 incident was shrouded in secrecy for decades; neither the crew of the *Rutherglen* nor relatives of the H5 crew were told the true cause of the tragedy.

During the conflict a number of Anglesey men found themselves in exotic locations they would never have dreamed of visiting, places such as the Holy Land. In March, *Y Clorianydd* published a letter from Private Griffith Williams of Capel Mawr who was in the land of Canaan:

> I received the Christmas parcel safely; everything had kept well; it took about three months to arrive. The people here live exactly like the stories in the Bible . . . They get up very early in the morning and they go to bed very early. . . . The men have three or four wives, and the women work to keep their husbands. Pretty good, isn't it? So the old 'codger' has a very easy life. There are three types of church near us, and they worship in different ways, but they have the same God as ourselves. . . . I hope that I can return soon to tell you the story.
> [Translated]

Back in home waters on 16 March, the 1,569-ton steamer *Rathmore*, belonging to the LNWR, was involved in a collision and sank about an hour after leaving Ireland for Holyhead. There were 720 persons on board; about 200 were said to have injuries such as broken limbs or dislocated joints. The number of deaths is uncertain; some sources claim 26 people died. The ship was later raised and continued in service. The following week, on 23 March, the 124-ton schooner *Jane Gray* was sunk by a U-boat off Pembrokeshire. There were no casualties. The captain of the *Jane Gray*, built in Amlwch in 1865, was Captain Hugh Lewis of Moelfre.

On account of the colossal damage inflicted by U-boats in the Irish Sea, the Irish Sea Hunting Flotilla was established in Holyhead. Lieutenant-Commander R. de Saumarez RN was appointed to organise an effective anti-submarine force. One of the ships deployed was HMS *Patrol*, under the command of Captain Gordon Campbell VC, DSO.

As the result of food rationing and the introduction of various regulations stipulating the prices of common foodstuffs and measures to counteract hoarding, it was perhaps inevitable that the courts would be kept busy dealing with people who had fallen foul of these rules. Even pillars of the community could find themselves in trouble. In late March, Lieutenant A.F. Pearson, a former High Sheriff of Anglesey and chairman of the local Magistrates Board, appeared in court in Holyhead on seven counts of breaching the Food Control (Hoarding) Order, 1917. He was alleged to have hoarded the large amounts of tea, sugar, jam and other foods which had been found at his house. The outcome was that the charges against him were dismissed. However, Thomas Williams, a farmer of Tyddyn Fadog, Llanfair Mathafarn Eithaf, was less fortunate when he appeared in another court a few weeks later. He was charged with selling adulterated (i.e. watered down) milk. Thomas Williams maintained in court that this was because the cows had been fed with straw because his supply of hay had run out. The court refused to believe his explanation and fined him £5.

On 1 April, the Royal Flying Corps (established in 1912 to operate aircraft for the Army) was amalgamated with the Royal Naval Air Service (established in 1914 to perform similar duties for the Navy) to form the Royal Air Force (RAF). The Women's Royal Air Force (WRAF) was formed at the same time. On the same day the 4,312-ton *Conargo* was sunk by a U-boat in the Irish Sea. There were a number of deaths but the survivors landed at Holyhead. The *Conargo* remained afloat but was later torpedoed again and sank 20 miles north-west of the Skerries. On 20 April, the 3,366-ton *Florrieston* was torpedoed and sunk by U-91 on route from Almeira to the Clyde with a cargo of copper ore; 19 lives were lost. The wreck lies about 6 miles north-east of South Stack (see Map 2, p. 32).

On 30 April, the 255-ton cargo steamer *Kempoch* (under Captain John Roberts of Morawelon, Moelfre) was attacked by gunfire from the German U-boat UB-85 when sailing from Belfast to Manchester with a cargo of potatoes. The *Kempoch* returned fire, but eventually the ship had to be abandoned. No lives were lost. The U-boat was later itself sunk by a naval patrol vessel. The U-boat commander, who survived the incident, stated that his vessel had received so much damage from the *Kempoch* that they could offer no resistance. As a result of the U-boat commander's evidence, Captain Roberts was awarded the Distinguished Service Cross. Captain Roberts received the award from King George V at a ceremony in Buckingham Palace on 29 June. Another Moelfre sailor, John Bloom Roberts (aged 15), must have considered himself very lucky – he should have been a crew member on the *Kempoch* but, by an extraordinary twist of fate, was unable to join the ship because he had suffered an accident. He heard about the incident at home in Moelfre.

In early May it was reported that in a meeting of Anglesey County Council, a certain Mr H.R. Davies suggested that a committee be appointed to consider the use of water power to produce electricity in North Wales. Mr Davies pointed out that after the war, industry and a modern post-war society would need large amounts of electricity and this would an effective way of producing it.

On 5 May, the sound of gunfire was heard in Holyhead and the surrounding area. A steamer called the *Pandora*, en route from Dublin to Garston, was being attacked by a German submarine. The *Pandora* was later towed into Holyhead.

Undeb Gweithwyr Môn was continuing the campaign to secure a fair wage for farm workers. They were demanding a weekly wage of 32*s* a week for workers who received their food on the farm and 44*s* for those who received no food at their place of work. On 21 May, about 1,000 workers paraded through Llangefni to draw attention to the demands of *Undeb Gweithwyr Môn*. An appearance by Ellis Jones-Griffith MP, who had expressed little sympathy for the workers' plight, was greeted with little enthusiasm. The District Wages Board fixed a rate of £1 11*s* 6*d* for workers receiving no food – much less than the union had hoped for.

On 18 May, forty-six Sinn Féin prisoners arrived at Holyhead on a warship. This was a time of some unrest in parts of Ireland. The following day they were transported from Holyhead by train to prisons in England. Among them was one woman, Countess Constance Georgina Markiewicz (1868–1927). She was an unusual figure – a product of the Anglo-Irish gentry who had immersed herself in nationalist politics in Ireland since 1908. She was escorted, together with her dog, to a first class railway carriage and taken to London. When she arrived at Euston, she was placed in a taxi and driven to Holloway prison.

On 24 May, the 423-ton *Red Rose* sank on a voyage from Littlehampton to Le Havre with a cargo of government stores. Four of the crew, Captain Pritchard, first mate W. Pritchard and seamen W. Roberts and H. Thomas, were from Amlwch and the town was anxiously awaiting news of their fate, but hopeful that all would be well. Both the *Chronicle* and *Y Clorianydd* reported this story but neither paper made any further reference to it in subsequent editions. However, their names appear on Amlwch's War Memorial; in fact, a total of twelve people died in the *Red Rose* incident.

It was announced that from 29 May, special permits would be needed by civilians travelling to Ireland. This was done in order to exercise more control over movements of people at Holyhead, where dubious people were still trying to make the journey on the ferry to Ireland.

On 30 May, three German prisoners of war escaped from an internment camp at Llangaffo but were later recaptured near Plas Coch, Llanedwen.

On 4 June, the motor schooner *Eilian* brought five survivors of a German submarine to Holyhead. The submarine had been sunk by a decoy vessel in Caernarfon Bay. Eight enemy submarines were sunk in the Irish sea during the first seven months of 1918. In actual fact, U-boat activity had decreased during the summer, which suggested that the efforts of the Holyhead Naval Base, the Hunting Flotilla and the Llangefni Airship Station were proving to be effective. In order to further boost the effectiveness of the Airship Station, eight Airco DH6 aircraft were deployed there from 6 June to 18 August. These were followed by a number of SS Zero airships which were equipped with powerful Rolls-Royce engines giving them greater speed and the ability to carry heavier, more powerful bombs.

In early June, Robert John Thomas of Garreglwyd, Holyhead, was awarded a baronetcy in recognition of 'his public service in respect of the North Wales Heroes' Memorial and his magnificent contribution of £20,000'. Robert John Thomas was a politician and shipowner of considerable wealth and a product of the Liverpool Welsh community. It was also announced that Gors House, Holyhead, was to be converted into a convalescent home for discharged and disabled soldiers, preference being given to Anglesey's own heroes. This facility was being provided by Sir Robert John Thomas, but would not be opened until 1919.

In early July it was announced that Captain Henry Thornbury Fox-Russell of the Royal Flying Corps (brother of the late Captain John Fox-Russell of Holyhead) had been awarded a Military Cross. The published citation for which the decoration was conferred stated:

> He formed one of a patrol [of aircraft] that silenced an enemy battery.
> He dropped bombs on to two of the guns, silenced others with his machine gun, and then engaged transport on a road. This operation was carried out under heavy fire and very difficult weather conditions. On another occasion he dropped bombs and fired 300 rounds on enemy trenches from a height of 100ft. His machine was then hit by a shell and crashed in front of our advanced position. He reached the front line, and while there saw another of our machines brought down.
> He went to the assistance of the pilot, who was badly wounded, extricated him under heavy fire and brought him to safety. He showed splendid courage and initiative.

On 14 July coupon books for rationing of meat, sugar, fats and lard were issued. This resulted in further court cases where retailers and others were charged with improper use of these coupons or for selling foodstuffs without asking for coupons. Application forms for ration books had been distributed in June; the log book of Llanddaniel Fab Primary School records that the school was 'closed for two days to enable teachers to distribute and collect application forms for ration books'.

On 15 July, the Second Battle of the Marne began and lasted until 5 August. An Allied force of French and American troops overwhelmed the Germans. It proved to be the last major German offensive on the Western Front. Back home in late July, one of the items discussed in a meeting of the Anglesey Education Committee was the employment of a man described as an enemy alien, William Jacob Fox Kalvin. Kalvin had been brought before a court in December 1914 on charges under the Aliens Registration Act (1914), but the case was dismissed (see Chapter 2). In the Education Committee meeting, a certain Mr H.O. Williams maintained that it was not fair to employ Mr Kalvin. This view was seconded by a Mr W. Owen. But the Revd J. Williams said he had known Mr Kalvin for a number of years and that the military authorities had not interfered with him. He maintained that Mr Kalvin should not be penalised because he was an alien. However, the committee voted to dismiss him.

Sunday 4 August was the fourth anniversary of the start of the war and this was remembered in many of the island's places of worship. St Seiriol's Church, Holyhead, made a collection for the work of the Red Cross and the vicar, the Revd T. Edwin Jones, said:

> On this fateful day of 4 August let us, while remembering and reverencing those who have fallen in the strife, also thank God that we have been roused from the total lethargy that was strapping our strength as a nation, and pray that never again shall we become as selfish, self-centred and unpatriotic as we were before the outbreak of war. One is inclined to think that the war will not last very much longer, and that probably before this date comes round again, this great world conflict will be practically over. . . .

Private Thomas Richard Owen of Coedana had kept a personal diary of events in the trenches over several months in 1918. He wrote of weary men, the grim conditions, the shelling and the deaths. In August 1918, he described how he was temporarily able to leave the trenches to work in the harvest in the French countryside:

> I was called and asked how much I knew about farming. So I was quite lucky to be sent to Harvest Camp to try to gather the corn harvest. The British have commandeered all the crops that are near the trenches. The French have had to retreat and leave it all. The corn is too close to the enemy and so it is too dangerous for them to gather it. . . . There are about 200 men here and many Welshmen. It is much better than being with the Battalion [in the trenches]. I write this on the anniversary of the war, on the morning of Sunday 4 August 1918. I am very lucky to be working here, but I would much prefer to come over to Anglesey. But thank goodness for being spared the trenches and being in the great battles. . . . [Translated]

Owing to increased military activity late in August, Thomas Richard Owen was forced to leave the harvest and resume duties with his battalion. On 2 September 1918, he was killed.

August 1918 saw a number of unfortunate accidents in Anglesey. On 9 August, a 28-year-old naval man called Josiah Tomlinson was travelling on a train between Gaerwen and Llanfair Pwllgwyngyll when he was observed to 'open the carriage door, step on the footboard and jump off the train' which was travelling at over 50mph. An inquest heard that he died of his injuries in Bangor Infirmary and that bottles of whisky were found in his pocket. Less than a fortnight later at the Llanddaniel Fab level crossing, Mrs Mary Williams and her 18-month-old child were injured after the child strayed into the path of a train. A few days later, 14 year-old Theophilus Griffiths of Beaumaris died in Bangor Infirmary after trying to jump onto a bus on the Menai Bridge to Beaumaris road. He slipped and fell under the back wheel.

In August it was announced that Gunner Hugh Roberts, Bodowen, Llanfaethlu, had received a Military Medal for 'gallant conduct on the occasion of a man in the detachment being mortally wounded and for previous good record'. Also in the same month, a fête was held in the grounds of Plas Penrhos, Holyhead, to raise funds for Holyhead Red Cross Hospital in Holborn Road. The event was attended by a number of well-known dignitaries, including Lord Sheffield (Anglesey's High Sheriff), the Bulkeley-Williams family, Sir Ellis Jones-Griffith MP and Lady Griffith and Sir Robert John Thomas. A sum of £550 was raised – a not inconsiderable amount at the beginning of the twentieth century.

Another Anglesey man who found himself in an exotic location was Richard Hughes of Highfields, Maeshyfryd Road, Holyhead. In August, a letter written by him in Palestine was published in the *Chronicle*:

> It is very hot here during the day, but towards night it becomes cold, and the flies – well, one doesn't know how to deal with them. When we were in the Holy City [Jerusalem], we went through the streets, our chaplain explaining everything to us as we went. We also visited the scenes of the Crucifixion. I am writing this letter under the welcome shade of a fig tree, which is easily the most popular tree in this land. Grapes are beginning to bloom here in plenty.

On 18 August the Bishop of Bangor consecrated the whole of the island of St Tysilio in Menai Bridge for public burial. Previously only part of the island had been used for this purpose, the remainder being used for agriculture. The Marquess of Anglesey had conveyed the whole of the island to the church. Three days later, painting work on the Menai Suspension Bridge was finally completed, having taken three months.

German prisoners of war were actively involved in large drainage schemes on the Malltraeth marsh (Cors Ddyga). By August 1918 they had dug two ditches on either side of the Cefni river all the way from Malltraeth to the post road (the A5) near Llangefni. The standard of their work was praised.

In a meeting of Holyhead Trades and Labour Council on 21 August, the matter of a fire siren was one of the items being discussed. It was claimed that when a haystack caught fire a few weeks earlier, a certain Mr Williams of the electricity works refused to sound the siren without first obtaining permission from the police. This was alleged to have caused a 1½ hour delay before a fire crew appeared at the scene.

In late August, a large garden fête was held at Baron Hill, Beaumaris. It was attended by 900 people and raised £180 for war charities. Assisting the fundraising, the queen and a number of notable figures were said to have donated items to be sold at the event.

Although fewer vessels were being sunk by U-boats in the Irish Sea, the attacks were still continuing. On 21 August, the 1,936-ton *Boscawen* was torpedoed without warning and sunk with the loss of one life by UB-92 when en route from Birkenhead to Barry. The wreck lies in Caernarfon Bay. The following day, the 1,352-ton *Palmella* was torpedoed and sunk by UB-92 while on a voyage from Liverpool to Lisbon with the loss of 28 lives. The wreck lies 25 miles north-west of South Stack (see Map 2, p. 32).

Allotments had become popular after about 1916 and in order to encourage horticultural skills, prizes were often awarded for the best allotments. On 22 August, Colonel R. Stapleton-Cotton presented prizes to allotment holders in Llanfair Pwllgwyngyll. A similar event was held at Amlwch during the same week.

In early September the LNWR announced that in consequence of the shortage of supplies, they would no longer be able to provide soap and towels in train lavatories. The *Chronicle* commented rather grumpily: 'This is a very belated statement seeing that travellers have suffered for a long time from this disability.'

In a Menai Bridge court on 2 September, John Albert Wells of Leicester was charged with being in possession of 'photographic apparatus' (in other words, a camera) in a prohibited area. He was observed by Police Sergeant Owen Roberts in the area between the suspension bridge and St George's Pier. Sergeant Roberts described his camera as 'a large one on a tripod stand'. When told that he was in a prohibited area, Wells replied that he was not aware of it. He was fined 15s. Sergeant Owen Roberts was obviously very adept at spotting cameras in prohibited areas as another case reached the same court only a few weeks later. On this occasion, Frank Sturdy of Knaresborough used his camera on the central span of the suspension bridge, with 'its lens directed towards the pier'. When asked for his permit, Sturdy replied that he did not know a permit was needed. He volunteered to destroy the exposed plate and did so immediately. He was found guilty and was fined a much more robust £2.

On 19 September, an exhibition of house plans was held in the Town Hall, Holyhead. New houses were seen to be a great necessity since existing houses were considered to be in poor condition and were insufficient in numbers. Sir Ellis

Jones-Griffith MP claimed that at least a thousand new homes were needed to satisfy the island's needs.

It was reported in September that Sir Robert John Thomas, the Holyhead philanthropist, intended to supply 50 tons of coal for distribution to the most needy in Holyhead during the winter of 1918/19. This came at a time when coal was becoming scarce. During the winter of 1917/18, Sir Robert had supplied 150 Holyhead people with coal.

On 30 September, Bulgaria signed an armistice to cease hostilities, to be followed by Turkey on 30 October. This signalled the beginning of the end. It was increasingly clear that the end of the war was in sight and an Allied victory was certain. In the 4 October edition, a *Chronicle* editorial proclaimed with considerable hyperbole:

> The war has reached its climax, and indeed there is every sign that the supreme crisis is approaching in the brilliant series of events which have unfolded themselves with such bewildering rapidity in the fortnight that has just elapsed. As offensive after offensive has been launched with such astonishing success in every theatre of war, the profound genius of allied strategy has revealed itself, and there are few indeed who would now be found to engage in niggling criticism of the conduct of operations....

In the same edition the *Chronicle* reported that King Haakon VII of Norway had awarded 'a piece of silver with an inscription' to Captain William John Hughes of Bronrallt, Brynsiencyn, for his gallant rescue of the captain and crew of the Norwegian vessel *Svendsholm* in March 1917.

Following heavy rain in the first week of October, the River Cefni flooded the Malltraeth Marsh. German prisoners of war from a nearby camp were called to carry out remedial work.

On 8 October, the people of Holyhead were invited to attend a 'startling lecture' given by a well-known writer, Mr William Le Queux, on the subject 'German Spies and their Methods'. Mr Le Queux's visit to Holyhead had been arranged by Sir Robert J. Thomas and proceeds were in aid of the North Wales Heroes' Memorial.

Shortly before 9 a.m. on Thursday 10 October 1918, the 2,646-ton Irish mailboat *Leinster* was sailing from Kingstown (Dún Laoghaire) to Holyhead with 771 people on board, made up of 180 civilians, 77 crew, 492 military personnel and 22 Irish postal workers who were sorting mail. Many of the military personnel (soldiers, sailors, nurses and airmen) were coming from, or going on leave. The ship was torpedoed twice by German U-boat UB-123 shortly after leaving Ireland and sank in a few minutes. 115 civilians and 37 of the crew, including the captain, died. All but one of the postal workers died. The total number of deaths was officially given as 501, which is the greatest ever loss of life in the Irish Sea. Ships like the *Leinster* were often escorted by airships or destroyers for much of the war in order to deter attacks by

U-boats. On this occasion, sadly, there was no escort. The *Chronicle* reported that Private Evan Roberts of Holyhead was a passenger on the *Leinster*; he was saved and taken to a Dublin hospital. However, Owen Richard Hughes and Private Owen Hughes, also of Holyhead, died in hospital in Dublin. The two men were described as 'victims of the huns'. Two Holyhead women, both of whom worked as stewardesses on the *Leinster*, also died. They were Hannah Owen and Louisa Parry. In Holyhead, which had already suffered a number of tragedies in the four years since the conflict began, the *Leinster* incident caused a feeling of shock and profound indignation. The funerals of those brought ashore in Holyhead were described in the press as a sombre affair. It was reported that business premises were closed and that large numbers had assembled along the route to witness the funeral procession. A relief fund for widows, orphans and others in Holyhead affected by the tragedy was immediately established; Sir Robert Thomas of Garreglwyd subscribed £500.

On 14 October the 794-ton *Dundalk*, on a voyage from Liverpool to Dundalk with general cargo and a number of passengers, was sunk by torpedoes from UB-123 and U-90 5 miles north-west of the Skerries, with the loss of 19 lives (see Map 2, p. 32). On the same day Llangefni Urban Council decided in view of the government's 'Household Fuel and Lighting Order' that the town's shops would have to close at 7 o'clock on Monday to Thursday and 8 o'clock on Saturdays.

In mid-October a travelling show of war films visited Newborough, Llangefni, Llannerch-y-medd and Amlwch with a lecture by a Mr Grieve of London. They were described as the best ever seen in Anglesey and the events were organised by the National War Aims Committee.

At the end of 1918, Anglesey was gripped by an influenza epidemic. This was a massive pandemic which claimed millions of lives worldwide. Anglesey schools were closed for a fortnight, while in Llanfair Pwllgwyngyll, two children in the Maes Garnedd children's home died. In Holyhead, influenza was described as 'rampant'; William Williams, his wife and two of their six children, John Thomas (aged 6) and Goronwy (aged 7 months) died within a few days of each other at the end of October. Their deaths caused great fear and distress in the town. The influenza returned in February 1919 and caused further misery.

At the end of October Sergeant Major Ernest Salt was awarded the Distinguished Conduct Medal (DCM) for gallantry on 22 August 1918. He was presented with a gold watch and chain at the Trygarn-Griffith Coffee House, Bodedern. In the same week a new Chief Constable of the Anglesey Constabulary was appointed. He was R.H. Prothero, who succeeded his father Lewis Prothero who had retired, aged 78.

On 1 November, a large crowd assembled in Market Square, Llangefni, to honour Seaman William Williams, originally from Amlwch, who had been awarded the Victoria Cross, as well as the Distinguished Service Medal with Bar and the French Médaille Militaire for conspicuous bravery on board the Q-ship *Pargust* which was involved in the sinking of U-boat UC-29 off Ireland in July 1917. Sir Richard Williams-Bulkeley thanked him for his valour and presented him with a gold watch and war bonds to the value of £120. The Clio band played 'See the Conquering Hero Comes' and the meeting closed with the National Anthem. William Williams' gallantry earned him celebrity status, although the details of his actions were not revealed as they had not been made public up to that time.

On 3 November, Austria-Hungary signed an armistice to bring hostilities to an end. A day later, the German High Seas Fleet at Kiel was in the hands of mutineers and on 8 November, a German delegation sought to discuss terms of surrender. On 10 November, the Kaiser (Wilhelm II) fled to the Netherlands and on the following day an armistice was signed bringing the 1,561-day war to an end at 11 a.m. The news was greeted with relief and joy. David Lloyd George was quoted as saying, 'We can confidently say that there will be no more wars.'

In the same week as the Armistice, Llangefni VAD Sewing Committee were still active and were sending a hundred warm garments including shirts, pyjamas and mufflers to naval prisoners of war. They intended holding a 'Sock Tea' in December in order to raise money to provide socks for prisoners of war belonging to the Royal Welch Fusiliers.

On the day the war ended, a 29-year-old Austrian-born soldier was recovering in hospital. Like so many who had fought for the enemy, he was convinced that his side was winning the war; when he heard news of Germany's surrender, he felt nothing but humiliation and anger. He, and many others, found defeat difficult to swallow, and they felt the need to blame someone. He believed that Jews and Socialists were responsible for Germany's downfall and felt that Germany had been stabbed in the back by people who became known as 'November Criminals'. This young soldier (who became a German citizen in 1932) was called Adolf Hitler; the seeds of a future conflict had already been sown.

In Anglesey, in early November, four bodies were washed on shore, one at Aberffraw and three at Llanfaelog. They were impossible to identify, having been in the water for some time, but it was believed they were from the *Leinster*. A number of bodies from the *Leinster* were also washed ashore in Ireland.

Victory day was 15 November 1918 when church bells rang out, work stopped and flags were everywhere. In Menai Bridge, there was a public meeting in the town square and according to the *Chronicle*, 'airships and aeroplanes appeared and the latter gave a fine exhibition of trick flying'. In the evening, 60 naval officers attended a dinner at the Victoria Hotel and there were fireworks on the pier. In Beaumaris, confirmation of the armistice was reportedly not received until about noon, but celebrations quickly followed. In Holyhead, news of the armistice arrived early in the morning. The sound of the hooters and whistles of ships in the harbour was heard all over the town and thanksgiving services were held in many of the churches and chapels.

At the end of November it was announced that Captain Henry Thornbury Fox-Russell of Holyhead (who had been awarded a Military Cross for bravery only a few months earlier) had died in a flying accident in Cheshire where he was working as an instructor.

In the November issue of the anti-war monthly *Y Deyrnas*, there were calls for conscientious objectors who had been imprisoned (such as the Revd Ben Meyrick) to be freed. It was claimed that 1,500 remained in prison, of whom 700 had suffered over two years of hardship. Releases came in early December for the crew of the *Saxon*, interned in Germany since August 1914, who returned to their homes. A number of them were from the Amlwch area. The *Saxon* was returned to its owners in the same month.

Other Anglesey men serving in the Merchant Navy were also held in internment camps by the Germans and were now being freed. R.J. Thomas (aged 33, of Hen Siop, Caergeiliog), a Second Engineer on the *Frankdale* was held at Ruhleben. R. Parry (aged 22, of 4 Trearddur Square, Holyhead) served on the *Brecknockshire* and was interned at Güstrow. W. Jones (aged 32, of 14 Salem Street, Amlwch) served on the *Mount Temple* and was interned at Brandenberg. R. Griffiths (of Elwy House, Amlwch Port) served on the *Esmeraldas* and was held at Ruhleben.

There was good news concerning Willie Williams of the Royal Welch Fusiliers, who had been missing since May 1918. In a telegram received in Holyhead, he related that he had been a prisoner of war since May and that he had arrived at Leith, Scotland, on 7 December. However, on the very same day, his mother was buried at Holyhead; she died without finding out her son was safe.

A general election was held on 14 December 1918. *Undeb Gweithwyr Môn* had called on Sir Owen Thomas to be a Labour parliamentary candidate for Anglesey and he agreed to stand as an Independent Labour candidate. The sitting Liberal MP, Ellis Jones-Griffith (who had represented Anglesey at Westminster since 1895) was the only other candidate. It was a close contest but the seat was won by Sir Owen Thomas with a majority of only 140. In Westminster, David Lloyd George continued as Prime Minister.

In the final edition of the *Chronicle* for 1918, an editorial commented:

> Once more Christmas may be a season of gladness. But the Christmas of 1918 is necessarily a time of commemoration. We know how many households have been hallowed by the supreme sacrifice made by one or more of its members. The coming season is consecrated in the minds and hearts of all of us. Yet it will be a season of gladness.

On a more parochial note, the *Chronicle* reported that in the final days of 1918, plans for a new reservoir at Menai Bridge were again activated, having been shelved in 1915 through lack of money.

CHAPTER SEVEN

THE AFTERMATH

At the end of the war, there were, of course, changes afoot. The Women's Land Army, the Land Girls, having performed their duties well, was no longer considered necessary after the hostilities ended. The organisation was disbanded during the course of 1919.

On 10 January 1919, the 229-ton *Calista* was sunk in the Irish Sea between the Isle of Man and Dublin while on a voyage from Preston to Dublin with a cargo of coal. Ten lives were lost. It is believed the ship may have struck a German mine. The wreck lies in 68m of water off the Calf of Man. Three Moelfre men, William Parry, Lewis Roberts and Owen Evans were among those who perished.

On 18 January, the Paris Peace Conference began and would last until January 1920. The dominant figures at the conference were Georges Clemenceau (France), David Lloyd George (Great Britain), Woodrow Wilson (USA) and Vittorio Emanuele Orlando (Italy). At the conference, treaties were prepared detailing peace terms with the enemy nations. The Treaty of Versailles (28 June 1919) is the best known; it was the treaty imposed by the Allies on Germany. Woodrow Wilson famously described the First World War as 'the war to end all wars' but it is thought that the author H.G. Wells had first used the phrase.

On 28 January, twenty repatriated prisoners of war were entertained to a 'pleasant social event, whist drive and dance' at Church House, Holyhead. Such events were held throughout the island. Other things were beginning to get back to normal too; in February, Rhosneigr railway station was reopened after being closed for two years. In the same month, members of Disgwylfa Presbyterian Chapel in Holyhead announced their intention to acquire a pipe organ worth £300 as a memorial to the fourteen members of the chapel who died in the war. Owing to the cessation of hostilities, the Beach Red Cross Auxiliary Hospital at Holyhead was closed in February and the few remaining patients were transferred to the Holborn Road Red Cross Hospital.

Influenza, which had struck the island's communities at the end of 1918, made an unwelcome return in February causing school closures and other disruption. This Spanish 'flu epidemic caused an estimated 50–70 million deaths worldwide, far more than the First World War. In Britain, it claimed 237,400 lives.

In the February edition of *Y Deyrnas*, there were renewed calls for the release of all conscientious objectors held in prison. Lloyd George was the man deemed responsible for their continued plight. An article described them as:

> . . . innocent men, men of good character, of above average intellect, conviction and honesty and their only crime is their belief that they should not kill their fellow men. . .
> [Translated]

By July 1919, all conscientious objectors were freed.

On Saturday 14 June 1919, the Lady Thomas Convalescent Home opened. The home catered for discharged and disabled soldiers and sailors; it had three wards and could cater for 38 men. The opening ceremony was performed by Mrs Lloyd George and was attended by a number of local dignitaries.

The fund established for the building of a War Heroes' Memorial and new science laboratories at the University College of North Wales, Bangor, was gathering momentum. The aim was to collect £150,000 for these two projects. Anglesey was divided into 10 districts, each with a £2,000 target. Holyhead collected nearly £3,000.

Despite the end of the war, the government was still keen to receive investments from the public in order to pay the country's debts. In 1919, new investments were offered to the public; they were called 'Victory Loans'.

On 19 July, the official peace celebrations were held nationwide. At Holyhead, a 10 a.m. service at Tabernacle Congregational Chapel was followed by a procession, teas at various schools and a cinema show. Thousands were said to have lined the route of the procession. Ex-servicemen were entertained at the Lady Thomas Convalescent Home.

The Llangefni Airship Station was decommissioned and passed to a body called the Government Disposal Board in 1920. Anglesey County Council bought the site; some of the buildings were used as a small hospital (the Druid Hospital) until the early 1940s. The other sheds and buildings were demolished.

Many Anglesey homes had lost a father, son or brother. The loss of a loved one would be felt for many years after the war had ended, but on a more practical level, the loss of a breadwinner would leave many a large family in financial distress. In Anglesey, army losses were 955 (1.87 per cent of the population); these losses were mostly on the Western Front – at sea the number of deaths is uncertain. However, the total death toll is in excess of 1,000, a high price for a small island. Holyhead's war memorial alone features 287 names (including four women, three of whom died in the *Connemara* and *Leinster* tragedies); Amlwch 61; Menai Bridge 49; Llangefni 36; Llannerch-y-medd 29. The Llangefni County School memorial lists 38 former pupils. Many of the island's war memorials were officially unveiled by Sir Owen Thomas MP. The war memorial in the cemetery of Bryn Du Chapel, near Llanfaelog, lists eleven names, but the last name

Holyhead's war memorial bears the names of nearly 300 men and women who died in the First World War.

The First World War memorial in the cemetery of Bryn Du Chapel, near Llanfaelog. The last name on the memorial was a mistake – the soldier in question (Richard Owen of Tŷ Newydd) was not killed in France but merely missing.

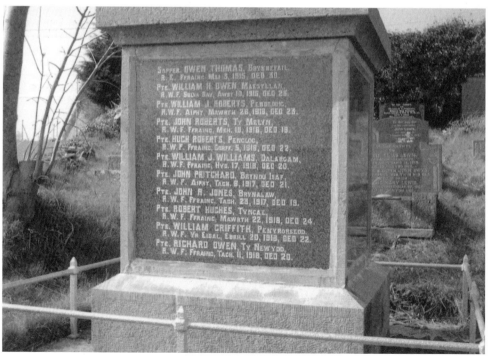

is apparently a mistake. The man was listed as having been killed on 11 November 1918, but in reality he was merely missing. This man, therefore, was able to read his own name on a war memorial!

And what happened to some of the personalities who emerged during the course of the war? Sir Owen Thomas fought and won another election to become Anglesey's MP again in 1922. Tragically, Owen Thomas lost three sons in the war (Owen Vincent Thomas, Trefor Thomas and Robert Newton Thomas). Owen Thomas died in 1923, aged 64, and is buried at Ebenezer Chapel Cemetery, Llanfechell. Sir Henry Jones died in 1922 and a museum bearing his name was established in the village where he grew up, Llangernyw, in 1934. It was opened by his friend, David Lloyd George.

The Revd John Williams of Brynsiencyn was awarded an honorary doctorate (and thus became a Doctor of Divinity) by the University of Wales in 1917. He died in 1921 and was buried at Llanfaes. The Revd Thomas Charles Williams of Menai Bridge, who had also encouraged young men to enlist, died suddenly in 1927. Distinguished scholar, Professor John Morris-Jones, of Llanfair Pwllgwyngyll died in 1921 and is buried at Llanfair Pwllgwyngyll. Anglesey's Member of Parliament from 1895 to 1918, Sir Ellis Jones-Griffith, died in 1926 and was buried at Llanidan Church, Brynsiencyn.

Sir Robert John Thomas of Garreglwyd, Holyhead, became Member of Parliament for Anglesey following the death of Sir Owen Thomas in 1923, but resigned in 1929. He was declared bankrupt in 1930 and died in 1951.

William Williams, hero of the *Pargust* and recipient of the Victoria Cross subsequently worked on ferries and later in a Holyhead dockyard. He died in Holyhead in 1965 and was buried at Burwen cemetery. The Amlwch road named Maes William Williams VC commemorates him. Captain Ellis Morris Roberts of the *Birchleaf*, who was snatched by a U-boat and interned in Germany, died in August 1936. Miss Jane Henrietta Adeane of the Stanley Sailors' Hospital was appointed a Dame of the British Empire for her war service; she died in October 1926, aged 84.

Mrs Mary Cornwallis-West, who had figured in the Kinmel Camp scandal, died in 1920. Her husband William Cornwallis-West, who had been deeply affected by the scandal, died in 1917. Patrick Barrett, the wounded soldier who became the subject of Mrs Cornwallis-West's attention and led to the Kinmel Park scandal, died in 1935, aged 46. After the war, imprisoned conscientious objector the Revd Ben Meyrick became Minister at Calfaria Baptist Chapel, Mynydd Mechell, in 1920 and stayed there until 1926.

Ifan Gruffydd of Llangristiolus served in the army throughout the conflict. He was wounded in September 1915 and brought home to recuperate before returning to the front. After the war ended he was not demobbed like most of his fellow soldiers because he had unwittingly enlisted for six years. He was sent to Egypt where he achieved the rank of Sergeant-Major. He chose not to follow a military career and returned to his native county. Ifan Gruffydd became well-known in Anglesey as a gardener, author

The War Heroes' Memorial at Bangor University was officially opened by Edward, Prince of Wales, on 1 November 1923.

and actor. Many people will remember him as caretaker of the County Offices at the Shire Hall, Llangefni. Ifan Gruffydd died in 1971.

In 1921, the Llanfair Pwllgwyngyll branch of the Women's Institute, established six years earlier, secured a building as a regular meeting place. This was a former army corrugated iron hut from the Kinmel Park camp. It was erected next to the toll-house and still stands there today, almost a century later. The man who helped establish the branch, Colonel R. Stapleton-Cotton, left Anglesey for Antigua in 1924 and died a year later, aged 76.

The people of Anglesey and the rest of North Wales had contributed generously to the North Wales Heroes' Fund at a time when there were many demands on public contributions and people generally had little money to spare. Finally, on 1 November 1923, the War Heroes' Memorial and the brown brick Science Memorial Building (now the School of Biological Sciences of Bangor University) on Deiniol Road, Bangor, were officially opened by Edward, Prince of Wales.

CHAPTER EIGHT

BETWEEN THE WARS

The war years had been a period of great prosperity for farmers in Britain, but the economic decline which followed saw a reversal in their fortunes. Prices received for agricultural products were not guaranteed from 1921 onwards; agricultural prices tumbled and wage rates in the industry were drastically cut. This led to increased poverty and unemployment. Housing conditions and the health of the people barely improved in the twenty years following the war. *Undeb Gweithwyr Môn* saw a decline in its membership and ceased to function as a separate organisation following its absorption into a larger nationwide union in 1929.

Even the upper classes did not escape the changes. In Anglesey, large estates such as Plas Newydd and Baron Hill sold some of their lands in 1920s and '30s in order to cope with higher taxation and death duties. Since the existing tenants bought most of these lands, the proportion of owner-occupied farms increased markedly between the wars.

In the General Election of 1929, Megan Lloyd George (daughter of David Lloyd George) was elected as Anglesey's Member of Parliament with a comfortable majority. She was among a comparatively small number of women MPs at Westminster; she continued to represent Anglesey in the House of Commons until after the Second World War.

Cinemas became an established feature of life by the 1930s and the 'talkies' became a regular and enjoyable pastime for many. During the 1930s the radio also became a popular means of entertainment and information. The opening of the medium-wave transmitter at Penmon in July 1937 brought better reception to listeners in Anglesey. By the outbreak of the Second World War, the radio was an established feature of many Anglesey homes.

The electricity network was gradually extended and the North Wales Power Company built a high voltage line across Anglesey in 1932, thus rendering the local electricity generating stations obsolete. By the end of the decade, Amlwch and Beaumaris, as well as the villages of Cemaes, Trearddur Bay, Rhosneigr, Pentraeth, Moelfre and Benllech, had been brought into the network. But at the outbreak of the Second World War, the paraffin lamp and the candle were still in use in many of the island's homes. The provision of mains water improved slightly, but no great strides were made in the two decades between the wars.

Car ownership also increased between the wars and the more comfortably-off middle class families could now afford their own private vehicle. However, they remained well beyond the means of the poor. The development of rural bus services from the 1920s onwards meant that travel became an easier option for those in areas not served by the railway network. The Crosville bus company took over many of these services from 1930.

Telephones also gradually became an established feature of life. Although few private homes were sufficiently privileged to have such a luxury, many businesses and offices acquired telephones. More significantly, the familiar red public telephone kiosks were to be found in the towns and most of the larger villages of Anglesey by the end of the 1930s.

At the end of the 1930s, agriculture was still the industry that formed the backbone of the island's economy. Other industries were few. It was a fragile economy with more than its share of unemployment and poverty; the depression had hit Britain hard during the 1930s and Anglesey had suffered more than most areas. During this period, unemployment rates for Anglesey were typically between 30 and 40 per cent. Some families found themselves forced to leave the island to seek employment elsewhere – indeed, between 1921 and 1939, the population of Anglesey fell from 51,700 to 46,000. The average income in 1939 was about £4 a week and the old age pension was about 10s. An average-sized house in Anglesey could be bought for £350. Thus, at the outbreak of the Second World War, Anglesey's economy was in decline and no particularly dramatic improvements in health and social conditions had taken place since 1918.

CHAPTER NINE

THE SECOND WORLD WAR – SETTING THE SCENE

When the First World War ended with Germany's defeat and surrender in November 1918, the Paris Peace Conference which began in January 1919 imposed severe terms on the defeated Germany. The Treaty of Versailles decreed that the border areas of Alsace and Lorraine were to become parts of France, other lands were to be handed over to Belgium and Poland and overseas German territories were to be lost. There was also to be a limit on the size of Germany's armed forces. In addition Germany was required to make sizeable reparations for the damage caused.

Forming a stable government in Germany proved difficult and settling the reparations was almost impossible. There was rampant inflation, rendering the German currency (the Mark) almost worthless. This was a breeding ground for unrest and the rise of Adolf Hitler and his Nationalsozialistische Deutsche Arbeiter Partei (or Nazi Party) was a direct consequence of this situation. Hitler and his party promised to make Germany great again; they won considerable popular support and in 1933 Hitler became German Chancellor. In 1934 he combined the offices of President and Chancellor and gave himself the title Führer. The Nazis then built up a huge army (Heer), navy (Kriegsmarine) and air force (Luftwaffe), collectively known as the Wehrmacht. He also formulated an agreement with Benito Mussolini, the fascist leader of Italy, to link their two countries (the Rome-Berlin axis). Throughout the 1930s the people of Europe feared that Germany's ambitions would start another war. The belief held by many Nazis that Jews and Socialists were largely responsible for Germany's surrender in 1918 resulted in action being taken against German Jews and later Jews in German-occupied Europe. This led to the horrific concentration camps and the events we now refer to as the Holocaust.

In 1938 the Nazis came into power in Austria and this led to the absorption of Austria into a 'Greater Germany'. Hitler then demanded that Czechoslovakia hand over Sudetenland, a border region with a substantial German population. Just as it seemed that conflict was inevitable, the international community yielded to these German demands (the Munich Agreement). War was averted for a short time, but few believed that a conflict could be totally avoided. In September 1938 the British

Conservative Prime Minister, Neville Chamberlain, visited Germany and came to an agreement ('Peace in our Time') with Hitler. In March 1939 Britain and France gave Poland a guarantee of military aid in the event of German aggression.

Germany demanded from Poland the town of Danzig (in Polish, Gdansk) as well as a road to East Prussia through the Polish Corridor (a former German land which had been given to Poland under the Treaty of Versailles to give the Poles access to the Baltic Sea).

Britain, fearing that a war might be inevitable, introduced conscription (the Military Training Act) a few months before the war began in May 1939. With the events of the First World War still imprinted on the minds of the people, the government were clearly not prepared to rely solely on volunteer enlistment. Rather ominously, Germany agreed a non-aggression pact with the Soviet Union in August 1939. After Poland refused the German demands, German troops marched into Poland on 1 September 1939 and Polish towns were bombed. This action led Britain and France to declare war on Germany on 3 September 1939. Thus began the bloodiest conflict in human history which was to last almost six years and claim an estimated 55 million lives worldwide.

CHAPTER TEN

THE HOME FRONT 1939–45

Aerial and Marine Activity

Aircraft must have been a comparative rarity in the period between the wars. However, as soon as the war began and the airfields at Valley, Mona and Bodorgan were constructed, the skies above Anglesey became very busy. Radar stations were also built, at Tywyn Trewan (near RAF Valley), Wylfa and South Stack. Youngsters in the area became adept at identifying different aircraft by the sounds of their engines. Most of these aircraft were of course British, but German aircraft did enter Anglesey's airspace quite frequently, especially in the earlier part of the war (1940–41). Sadly, there were to be a considerable number of aircraft accidents on the island and in the sea around it, some involving fatalities (see Map 3, p. 107). There were nearly 100 aircraft accidents involving deaths, injuries or serious damage, almost all involving Allied aircraft, although not all were stationed at Anglesey's airbases. About a quarter of these incidents involved aircraft crashing or ditching in the sea. The total number of deaths was almost 80, including 11 rescuers and 3 civilians. There are a few instances of German aircraft being shot down or crashing on Anglesey or in the sea near the coast.

There was also damage to property in Llanfair Pwllgwyngyll, Pentre Berw, Bodffordd, Llanfachraeth and Holyhead (by German aircraft) and Cemaes and Beaumaris (by British aircraft).

Considerable activity was taking place at sea. Holyhead harbour was used by a number of different vessels (including those importing explosives) and villages on the east coast of Anglesey were witness to considerable maritime activity to and from Liverpool.

Air raid precautions

Britain had been bombed on only a very small scale in the First World War, but with the development of faster aircraft with longer working ranges, the government expected that enemy bombing would be a major feature of any new conflict. The

British government estimated that there could be as many as 1 million casualties and 3 million refugees in the first month of the Second World War. It was also expected that London would be largely destroyed. After war was declared, the government immediately ordered 1,000,000 coffins, though thankfully the reality was nowhere near as bad.

Although much of Anglesey was rural and therefore not expected to be the target of aerial bombardment, there were some areas that were seen as more vulnerable than others. Holyhead, with its harbour and extensive railway sidings, would have been perceived as one of the most likely places to be bombed in Anglesey. Holyhead had no fewer than 16 public air raid shelters; one of these is preserved in Holyhead's Maritime Museum. The smaller town of Menai Bridge had four shelters. However, bombs could, and occasionally did, land anywhere on the island. In the most vulnerable areas, windows would be taped to reduce the danger from flying glass in the event of a bomb blast. Stirrup pumps were stored in some locations so that fires caused by bombs could be extinguished.

At night a blackout was imposed by law. Street lamps were unlit and houses were not permitted to show any light whatsoever. This meant that curtains had to be replaced by coarse black cloth called blackout material. Those who breached the blackout regulations could face a fine, exactly as they had done in the First World War. A local warden would remind those who did not fully conform to the blackout regulations.

A Morrison table shelter was issued to households in order to safeguard families against the possible collapse of their house in an air raid. This was a reinforced metal table with wire mesh sides which would be assembled inside a room, often the kitchen. It was possible for a family to enter the shelter and survive in the event that their house was attacked by bombs. On the other hand, the much larger Anderson shelter was erected in the garden and was dug in and surrounded by soil. In certain areas Anderson shelters were provided free of charge to families where the total annual income was less than £250; everyone else paid £7.

Air Raid Precautions were in the hands of local wardens of whom there were about 1.4 million throughout Britain. They were unpaid part-time volunteers who had other jobs during the day. They were provided with a basic uniform including a steel helmet bearing the letters ARP and they were trained in fire-fighting and first aid to enable them to keep an emergency situation under control until help arrived.

Censorship

During the war, details of troop movements, allied casualties and other matters were heavily censored. The media themselves were also reluctant to report matters which may have damaged the nation's morale. Consequently German aerial attacks in Anglesey (which happened on about 30 separate occasions during 1940 and 1941) went largely unreported by the local press, although such news spread rapidly by word of mouth (see Map 4, p. 113). Bomb damage which occurred between October 1940 and March 1941 at Holyhead, Pentre Berw and Llanfair Pwllgwyngyll was not properly reported in the *Anglesey Chronicle* until October 1944, some 3½–4 years later!

Evacuees

On 1 September 1939 pre-determined government plans (Operation Pied Piper) were implemented to evacuate children from areas thought to be most likely to suffer enemy bombing. These were mostly cities and areas near to military establishments. The evacuation was not compulsory, but such was the fear of bombing, most children from such areas were evacuated. Since Anglesey and North Wales generally were mostly rural, a large number of evacuees found their way to this area. Three Merseyside secondary schools evacuated pupils to Anglesey: Alsop School to Holyhead (540 pupils), Oulton School to Llangefni (300 pupils) and Blue Coat School to Beaumaris (240 pupils). Anglesey had been led to expect about 600 primary school evacuees but in fact nearly 2,500 actually arrived. Most of these were also from Liverpool or Manchester and they would arrive here by train with their gas masks slung over their shoulders.

Some of the evacuated youngsters would be educated in premises such as chapels, but others were educated in local schools using a 'double shift' system, local children in the morning and evacuees in the afternoon. In fact, no enemy bombing of any sort occurred in the first months of the war and by January 1940 it is estimated that some 40 per cent of evacuees had returned home. Evacuations occurred at other times during the conflict but the massive 1939 evacuation was the only large-scale government-organised evacuation of the war. Towards the end of the conflict, evacuees from the south-east of England (which was being terrorised by the V1 and V2 rockets) came to Anglesey in smaller numbers.

Foreign Servicemen

The Royal Dutch Navy was based at Holyhead for a time during the war. The Maritime Museum (previously the old lifeboat hut) was used as a canteen for a platoon of Royal Dutch Merchant Marines. Three Dutch ships were anchored there at various times during the war: a hospital ship, a supply ship and the third ship was used as quarters for the seamen. The Dutch captain lived at Llys y Gwynt in Llanfawr Close, where members of the Dutch royal family (who were in exile in Britain during the war) were occasionally entertained. The Stanley Hospital on Salt Island was staffed by both British and Dutch doctors and nurses. In St Cybi's Church there is a plaque to commemorate the Dutch presence in Holyhead during the war.

After the USA entered the war in late 1941, American servicemen became a familiar sight in Anglesey since RAF Valley was used by the large American bombers. The GIs were not always well liked by British servicemen as their pay was 8–10 times that of a British soldier; in 1943 American servicemen earned about $50 a month. There were one million GIs in Britain by the end of 1942.

Fundraising Campaigns

These were events organised on a national basis to raise money for the war effort by selling National Savings Certificates, Defence Bonds and other government investments. National Savings Stamps were sold to schoolchildren on a regular basis. There were several campaigns during the conflict; in general they were very successful. It has to be remembered that the First World War had been very costly to Britain and the 1930s was a time of great depression and poverty; in 1939 the country was hardly in a healthy position to fight another costly war. Loans from the public were an absolute necessity. The people of Anglesey raised huge sums despite being one of the poorest areas of Britain. The total raised in Anglesey during the war was in excess of £2.1 million.

Lord Haw-Haw

Those who lived through the war years will surely remember the radio broadcasts of William Joyce, better known as Lord Haw-Haw. Joyce was Irish by blood but had been born in the United States, though he held a British passport. In 1939 he began broadcasting from Hamburg and his catchphrase 'Germany calling, Germany calling' became well-known to the British public. The purpose of his broadcasts was simply to cause fear and anxiety. He often mentioned specific targets for possible German bombing; the bridges across the Menai Straits were mentioned in one of his broadcasts. His identity remained a mystery for much of the war and there was considerable speculation as to his identity. He spoke English with such a peculiar accent that identifying his nationality proved well nigh impossible. It is estimated that 6 million people listened to his preposterous propaganda, more for entertainment than anything else. After the fall of Germany in 1945, his broadcasts stopped and Joyce fled. He was eventually caught and brought to trial in London; he was found guilty of treason and was hanged in 1946.

Gas Masks

Fearing that the Germans would use poison gas, the population of Britain was issued with gas masks. Issuing one to every man, woman and child in the country was a huge undertaking. There were different versions for babies and toddlers. The gas

Members of the public as well as servicemen were expected to carry their gas masks at all times. Here Tegerin Lewis Jones of Menai Bridge wears his Army uniform with the gas mask in the bag over his shoulder, November 1940.

masks came in a cardboard box and had to be carried wherever one went. They had an unpleasant rubbery smell. Schools would routinely conduct gas mask drills during the school day.

Posters

Posters issued by government departments became a feature of life during the war. These were a form of propaganda encouraging people to join the armed forces, become land girls, grow vegetables and a host of other things. Various cartoon characters such as Dr Carrot and Potato Pete were used to get the message home to the younger generation.

Recycling metals

Early in the war all surplus metal was gathered so that it could be recycled and used for building tanks and aircraft. Pots and pans were often used and railings were often removed from houses, other buildings and even graves. The removal of railings was most unpopular; householders were not keen to have their houses damaged in this way, and religious leaders saw the removal of railings from chapels and churches as desecration.

Rationing

Rationing was introduced early in the war to deal with expected food shortages caused by attacks on ships bound for the United Kingdom. Each person would register with local shops and would be provided with a ration book containing coupons. When purchases were made, the purchaser had to give the shopkeeper the money and the coupon necessary. Shortages became commonplace and some items were almost impossible to obtain. Children were astounded and heartbroken to discover that sweet shops, previously well-stocked with delights, were almost empty! Chocolate bars, for example, became scarce and could only be enjoyed occasionally.

The British people were forced to accept new food items such as Spam (which came from America following the Lend-Lease Act of March 1941), and Snoek (a canned fish from South Africa). Various concoctions were devised by the Ministry of Food, such as Woolton Pie (named after Lord Woolton and containing various vegetables such as potatoes, cauliflower, carrots and onions) and the unpopular National Loaf (made from wholemeal flour with added vitamins). Interestingly, vegetables were never rationed but their prices were controlled and they were often difficult to obtain. Because the people's diet changed during the war years, the population was much fitter and healthier in 1945 than they were in 1939.

Clothes rationing was introduced in 1941. In order to conserve materials the government also introduced Utility Clothing and Utility Furniture in the last two years of the war. Many items remained on ration long after the war; rationing finally ended in 1954.

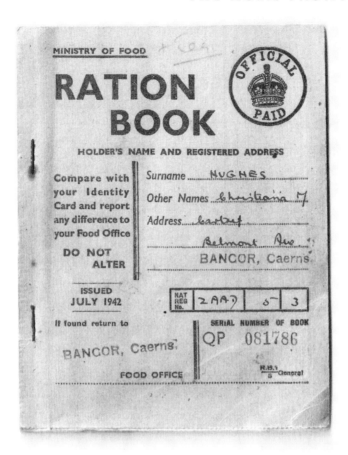

War Agricultural Committees

It is estimated that before the war Britain imported about 60 per cent of its food. In the event of war, the government was expecting that there would be attacks on British ships as had occurred in the First World War. It would therefore be necessary to produce more food in Britain, and so this is why allotments were encouraged. They were to be found in most parts of Anglesey as the island embraced the campaign 'Dig for Victory'. The importance of farming to the nation's survival was recognised when the War Agricultural Committees started work immediately at the outbreak of war on 3 September 1939.

Anglesey's 'War Ag' committee (up to a dozen in number, under the chairmanship of Sir Wynne Cemlyn Jones) was composed of farmers, representatives of farm workers and the Land Army (see p. 89). The committee was based in the County Offices in Llangefni where new single-storey accommodation was built next to the original Shire Hall building. These buildings and others erected later during the war were demolished in late 2008.

The role of the War Agricultural Committee was to tell farmers what was required of them in terms of production of various crops and to ensure that farmers were able to source all the feedstuffs, fertilisers and machinery they needed. The committee was able to hire tractors and other machinery to farmers for a fee. They were even able to hire prisoners of war to farmers for about £2.50 a week. The prisoners themselves, however, could only expect to earn 1*d* per hour for a 40-hour week. In short, the purpose of the War Agricultural Committee was to coordinate farming activity in order to maximise efficiency in producing that which was needed by the country as a whole.

Anglesey's War Agricultural Committee sent letters to the island's farmers and landowners early in September 1939 telling them what was required of them. The demands on farmers were very stringent and the penalties for not complying were severe. During the war there were a few cases where production at a particular farm was deemed to be unacceptably low and the farm would be taken over by the committee. At the beginning of the war about 14,500 acres of agricultural land in Anglesey were ploughed to produce food and by 1944 this had risen to 52,500 acres. Food was being grown literally everywhere – even the golf course at Plas Newydd had been ploughed for food production.

By 1943 it is estimated that 70 per cent of the nation's food was actually grown in Britain and the number of women in the Land Army was well over 80,000.

Invasion

At the beginning of the war there was much talk of a German invasion and steps were taken to block any possible routes. Although one might logically have expected an invasion to have been launched in the south or east of England, an invasion elsewhere could not be completely ruled out. In Anglesey, the wide open expanse of Red Wharf Bay was covered in stakes driven deep into the sand so that tanks and other vehicles could not reach land. In Holyhead, Salt Island and the Newry Beach area were festooned with barbed wire and gun emplacements. There were also numerous pillboxes on Holy Island, both in and around Holyhead and also in Trearddur Bay. This was to protect the area from a German invasion from the Irish Sea, which was considered possible for a time during the conflict. Some of the Holyhead pillboxes, such as the ones near the breakwater, were adaptations of existing structures; others were specially built using local stone and are still standing today. There are also pillboxes in the Llangadwaladr area and near the Bodorgan airfield since the wide Cefni estuary at Malltraeth was also considered a possible invasion point. An anti-tank block was installed near the A4080 at Malltraeth; this installation could prevent enemy tanks gaining access to local roads. There are also pillboxes in the Pentre Berw area. The coastal roads of Anglesey were routinely patrolled so that any invading forces could be detected.

The remains of an anti-tank block at Malltraeth. This was designed to prevent enemy tanks reaching the main road in the event of an invasion.

Women's Land Army

The need to produce food at home was the reason why the government formed the Women's Land Army in July 1939. Because men would be compulsorily called up for war service, there would be fewer agricultural labourers available to work the land. Additionally, in Anglesey many farmworkers were drawn to various construction projects such as the Tŷ Croes camp or RAF Valley where the pay was better. Therefore the Women's Land Army became a very important feature of wartime Anglesey, and Land Girls became a familiar sight on the island's farms.

About a third of the Land Girls came from the large cities and probably knew precious little about agriculture. Working on the land was hard work and the Land Girls were expected to turn their hand to virtually every aspect of farming. The pay was poor (£1.12 a week at the beginning of the war although this more than doubled by the end of the conflict) and the hours were long – 14 hours a day during the harvests. Most of the Land Girls lived on the farms where they worked, although some lived in hostels; there were hostels for Land Girls at Menai Bridge, Valley and Llannerch-y-medd. Surprisingly perhaps, the Women's Land Army lasted until 1950 – an indication that even after the war, Britain still needed to produce as much food as possible at home.

Women in the Armed Forces and Emergency Services

The Women's Royal Naval Service (Wrens) had over 70,000 women by the end of the war, although they were not permitted on board ships on active service. Instead, they were involved in loading torpedoes onto submarines, maintenance work, communications, weather forecasting and a number of other skills in naval bases in Britain and abroad.

The Women's Auxiliary Air Force (WAAF) was formed in 1938 and during the war had over 180,000 members. Although women were not allowed to go into combat, some were trained to fly and were used to transport aircraft from the factories to the airfields. Others were trained in various skills such as radar operation, packing parachutes, aircraft mechanics, weather forecasting and interpreting aerial photographs of enemy targets.

The women's branch of the army was known as the Auxiliary Territorial Service (ATS). It was formed in 1938 and grew to over 200,000 during the course of the war. They were not sent into combat or allowed to use firearms. They did their basic training in army camps, after which they underwent training to become drivers, telephonists, clerks, cooks, etc. Some women were used as anti-aircraft crews who spotted enemy aircraft so that they could be shot down.

The women of the Women's Voluntary Services (WVS) were always at hand to help with the hardship caused by bombing by operating mobile canteens, delivering water in tankers, distributing clothing, housing evacuees and many other things.

With the war came the need to manufacture aircraft, ammunition, bombs and other supplies. Many married women were employed in industry because they could not join any other women's service on account of their children. They started working in factories to an unprecedented degree – by June 1940 it is estimated that over 5 million women were in employment. On 18 December 1941 the National Service (No. 2) Act was passed; this allowed the conscription of unmarried women aged between 20 and 30 into the armed forces or vital war work. In the spring of 1942 this was extended to 19-year-old women. By 1943 it was estimated that 7.5 million women were in employment. In 1944 women in the armed forces numbered some 450,000.

Perhaps one of the most obvious roles for women in wartime was nursing. During the war more nurses were hurriedly trained. Some were sent to field hospitals overseas. A number of women were also trained as Air Raid Wardens (see above). In fact women played a massive part in the war effort. Traditionally many women were simply expected to be housewives and raise a family, and this was particularly true in Wales where traditional Nonconformist values were still strong in the 1930s.

CHAPTER ELEVEN

1939

At the outset of the Second World War, Anglesey was one of the poorest areas of the United Kingdom. The island's largest community, Holyhead, saw itself as a forgotten town, battling against the effects of deep recession and chronic unemployment. Some Holyhead men (as well as others from the seafaring communities of Moelfre and Amlwch) had joined Norwegian whaling vessels in the Antarctic simply because there were no local jobs. During the war, however, Holyhead and Anglesey generally was to spring into life with new industries and the presence of servicemen from all over the world. In Holyhead, a small naval base would be established on Parry's Island and Bryn y Môr. The Parry's Island base (situated between Turkey Shore Road and the Inner Harbour) consisted of a number of brick buildings and huts including a sick bay and a cinema.

The war would bring great pain and tragedy, but the economic fortunes of Holyhead and Anglesey generally would be enhanced during this period; wartime production greatly reduced unemployment and agriculture was boosted, although there were doubtless those in the community who did not benefit. In December 1939 a prominent Holyhead public figure remarked rather cynically, 'You cannot get anything for Holyhead unless you have a war.'

There was feverish talk of war in the national, regional and local papers long before the outbreak of hostilities on 3 September. In July 1939, local cinemas (such as the Arcadia in Llangefni) were showing a film called *The Warning* which described what might happen in the event of an air raid. In the same month it was reported that Newborough had completed its arrangements for the billeting of evacuees. Evacuation committees were established in all areas and they were given an indication of how many evacuees to expect. The committees then prepared their own billeting arrangements.

Also in July it was reported that a search for an anti-aircraft range had located a site at Ty'n Lôn, described as being 'between Aberffraw and Bodorgan' (see Map 5, p. 125). Although many Anglesey people were uncomfortable with the presence of airfields which they perceived as targets for enemy bombing, others saw such developments as a means of reducing the island's high level of unemployment. The airfield (later known as RAF Bodorgan) would be built in 1940 (see Chapter 12).

The Thetis *beached at Traeth Bychan.*

Opposite: The Thetis *Memorial at Maeshyfryd Cemetery, Holyhead.*

Those living in Anglesey at this time will recall the *Thetis* tragedy of 1 June 1939. The *Thetis* was a 275ft submarine, launched in June 1938, which was undergoing trials in Liverpool Bay with 103 men aboard. Tragically, the vessel sank and all but four of them were to perish in the accident. The *Thetis* was grounded at Traeth Bychan, near Moelfre on Sunday afternoon, 3 September, and was later towed away to Holyhead where the slow, unpleasant task of identifying the bodies was undertaken.

On Friday 29 September there was a funeral at Holyhead for 23 of the victims with Anglican, Catholic and Nonconformist clergymen taking part. The work of removing and identifying bodies, however, was still continuing. The *Thetis* was later salvaged and in 1940 was refitted as the *Thunderbolt*, which unfortunately went on to be sunk by an Italian vessel in March 1943. There is a remembrance service at the *Thetis* Memorial in Maeshyfryd Cemetery in June every year in memory of those who died in the tragedy. Holyhead Maritime Museum has artefacts from the *Thetis* on display.

Local papers of the period often contain interesting and intriguing little snippets. On 4 August 1939 the *Chronicle* printed a small paragraph about an acclaimed young actress called Karin Evans who lived in Germany. It seems that her father Hugh Jones Evans (described as a lecturer living in Berlin in 1939) was born in Beaumaris! One month later the war began and Berlin would hardly be the best place for a Welshman and his daughter when hostilities were declared. So what became of them? In fact, the film and theatre career of Karin Evans in Germany, which started in the late 1920s, continued through the war years and for many years beyond. She starred in about twenty German films from the 1920s to the 1960s and became a respected and distinguished stage actress. She died in Berlin in 2004, aged 95.

The last National Eisteddfod before the war, held at Denbigh in the first week of August, was something of a disappointment. Although the competitions were generally well supported, the Chair and the Crown had to be withheld because none of the entries was deemed to have reached a sufficiently high standard.

On 18 August, it was reported by the *Chronicle* that two young men from Holland (19-year-old law student Donald Gilhuys and Roelof van der Heide, an 18-year-old medical student, both of Amsterdam University) passed through Holyhead on a walking trip through Britain and Ireland. One wonders whether they were able to reach their homeland before war was declared. In the same edition, the *Chronicle* printed a small paragraph about the 1939 Radio Show where television was being demonstrated; the *Chronicle* described it as 'of academic interest since there is no prospect of this area enjoying the wonders of sight broadcasting'.

In August the Emergency Powers (Defence) Act was passed. This act gave the government powers to make any regulation it felt necessary for the defence of the country, maintaining public order, maintaining public services, public safety and so on. This was one of the most wide-ranging pieces of legislation ever passed in parliament; thousands of rules and regulations were made under the Emergency Powers Act throughout the war.

On 1 September, an appeal was launched by government minister Lord Woolton for half a million blankets for children who had been evacuated. It seems there was a shortage of blankets because the army had purchased all the available supplies. The public were urged to hand over the blankets at their local post office for free delivery. In the event they were not used, they would be returned.

When war was declared on Sunday 3 September 1939, a sombre nation listened to Neville Chamberlain's famous radio broadcast. The outbreak of war was not a surprise, but it was a profound disappointment for an apprehensive nation that war had not been averted. A general mobilisation of the armed forces and the evacuation of children from the cities began the same day as the country faced an uncertain future. In the City Cinema, Bangor (much frequented by Anglesey cinema-goers), the aptly titled film *Trouble Brewing* starring comedian George Formby was being screened.

A nationwide blackout was imposed immediately. This meant that householders had to ensure that not the slightest chink of light was visible from windows and doors.

Local Anglesey retailers were quick to advertise the availability of blackout material – priced from 9*d* a yard. In the streets the blackout meant that street lamps were turned off and there was no light in shop windows. People were not allowed to carry torches (even if they could buy any batteries) or even light a cigarette. Outside the towns, the blackout made no difference; villages did not have any street lamps until after the war.

Petrol rationing also began immediately; private motorists were allowed sufficient petrol for about 200 miles of motoring per month. Driving tests (which were established only a few years before the war) were also suspended. They were not reinstated until November 1946. Curiously, car radios (a rarity in 1930s Britain) were also banned but were permitted again before the end of the war.

Another government ruling closed theatres and cinemas and stopped events such as football matches where large gatherings could be expected. This was done because the government was certain that large-scale enemy bombing would occur as soon as war was declared. When this did not happen, cinemas, theatres and other events were again permitted since it was felt that they were a morale-booster.

The Welsh-language national weekly *Y Cymro* (*The Welshman*), in its first edition after the declaration of war, stated:

> For the second time in a quarter of a century, war has been declared between Great Britain and Germany. . . . The first few days of war were a strange experience. Thousands of mothers and children were moved from the large cities of England to Wales, where families were very willing to give sanctuary to strangers who are very different to us in their temperament and often in their conduct. Sand bags, ditches and blacked-out windows are very contrary to our values, and it was on our Sabbath that the God of War chose to appear with his arrogance and might. [Translated]

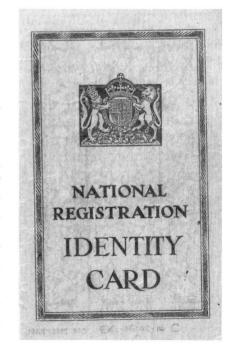

In 1939 the National Registration Act of 5 September required every individual (adults and children) to provide personal details; this was compulsory. Identity cards would then be issued. A certain Ifan Pugh of Colwyn Bay wrote a letter to the *Chronicle* urging the people of Wales to use the Welsh-language version of these forms. By early October it was reported that 46 million people were receiving these cards – a considerable logistical feat in a pre-computer age! The information provided would also be used to provide ration books.

Because conscription into the armed forces was introduced immediately, the question of persuading young men to volunteer did not arise. Therefore, unlike the First World War, far fewer strong local personalities emerged to argue the case for and against the war. The question of volunteering for service, or the reluctance to do so, was less evident in the local press. The rules did allow for exemption granted by a military tribunal and for conscientious objectors.

In the first week after the declaration of war, life continued much as before. The expected German air raids did not materialise and it was reported that British planes flying over Germany had not dropped bombs but 6 million leaflets. However, the war at sea began immediately and by 8 September it was reported that two British and two German vessels had been sunk. German air reconnaissance was reported over the east coast of England.

On 10 September a British expeditionary force moved into France where, together with French troops, they awaited a possible German attack, while the follwing day, Monday 11 September, it was reported that 50 Germans (26 men, 17 women and 7 children) had landed in Holyhead from Ireland (which remained neutral throughout the war) on their way to their own country. They were interned at Holyhead railway station for 24 hours before being sent by train to London, accompanied by armed guards. Their subsequent fate was not reported, but it is likely they were sent by ship to a neutral country and from there to Germany.

In the first month of the blackout the number of people killed in road accidents almost doubled. Since this was clearly unacceptable, the blackout regulations had to be eased a little. Pedestrians were now permitted to use a torch provided two sheets of tissue paper were placed over the bulb and the beam was directed downwards. Inevitably perhaps, there were to be breaches of the lighting regulations. In late

These three Menai Bridge brothers served in different capacities during the Second World War. Dr Islwyn Jones (left) was a chemist who worked in a government research establishment; Tegerin Jones (centre) served in the Army Pay Corps and subsequently in local government; Edward Maldwyn Jones (right), a pharmacist, travelled extensively with the Army during and after the conflict.

September two Holyhead residents (in Victoria Terrace and Maesydref) were fined 10s after being found guilty of breaching the regulations. Throughout the war there would be dozens of such cases in the courts.

On Wednesday 27 September, the Chancellor of the Exchequer Sir John Simon delivered his first wartime budget. Inevitably there were increases in virtually every tax, including income tax and duties on alcoholic drinks. The price of sugar was increased by one penny a pound.

Everyone had to adapt to wartime conditions and advertisers lost no time in using the war to their advantage. The company who manufactured the pain remedy Aspro ran an advertisement in September describing how an ARP warden was helped through a crisis by Aspro and how the same drug stopped the pain after another man lost his arm. In the following month and only seven weeks after the declaration of hostilities, North Wales furniture retailer Astons (with branches at Bangor and Caernarfon) were advertising a sale of 'pre-war furniture'. Throughout the war many advertisers made references to the conflict in order to sell their products.

Fryars (a large house with land built on the site of the old friary at Llanfaes, near Beaumaris) was requisitioned in September 1939 and taken over by Saunders-Roe (a British aero and marine engineering company) and a factory erected in the grounds for the conversion of flying boats. The house itself was used as office accommodation.

The former Saunders-Roe site at Llanfaes. The doors on the building provided access to a slipway, which has become overgrown with the passage of time.

The remains of the slipway leading from the former Saunders-Roe works at Llanfaes, near Beaumaris. In the distance, on the left, stands Fryars, where the offices were located.

Flying boats were ideal for long-range reconnaissance and useful for escorting convoys of ships. Since they also carried bombs, they could be used effectively against U-boats. These twin-engined aircraft were built in the USA by Consolidated Aviation, but had to be adapted for RAF use by installing suitable machine guns, radio equipment, bomb racks and so on. The RAF called them Catalina flying boats. They had very large fuel tanks and had a flying range of 2,500 miles. During the course of the war about 300 Catalinas were modified and prepared for RAF use at Llanfaes. Normally they were brought by ship from the USA to Largs in Scotland before being flown to Anglesey. At Saunders-Roe repairs were also carried out on the Catalinas as well as the four-engined Short Sunderland flying boats. The factory also manufactured other equipment for the war effort.

Saunders-Roe was originally based in the Isle of Wight but it was feared that this would be an easy target for bombs. Many of the Saunders-Roe staff moved from the Isle of Wight to Anglesey and remained there for the duration of the war. Initially the site had two hangars and some workshops. In August 1941 a hangar belonging to the company at Cowes was dismantled, brought to Beaumaris and reassembled on the site, while another hangar was added in December 1941. Saunders-Roe provided much-needed employment in this part of Anglesey for the duration of the war and for many years afterwards (under a variety of names including Cammell Laird and Faun).

Other Anglesey buildings were used by the forces during the war (see Map 5, p. 125). Plas Llanfair at Llanfair Pwllgwyngyll was commandeered by the army and used by various regiments. When a Scottish regiment was housed there, they occasionally marched through the village playing bagpipes. It was later occupied by American troops.

One of the finest houses in Anglesey, the magnificent mansion of Baron Hill in Beaumaris (which had not been occupied by the Williams-Bulkeley family since the 1920s), was used by the Royal Engineers, the Welsh Guards and other regiments at various times. It was also used as a centre for Polish servicemen and as a small military hospital. There was a fire in Baron Hill during this period and this, together with the theft of lead from the roof, began the sad decline of a once beautiful mansion (built in 1776) into the total ruin which it has now become.

Plas Penrhos (on Holy Island) was also occupied by the army. There was a recuperation hospital at Parciau in Marianglas for much of the war which catered mostly for servicemen, but in September 1943 some children from Lewisham in London came there for a three-week stay. Variety shows, performances by choirs and other entertainment were held there regularly. There was another hospital at Cemaes (Gadlys Auxiliary Hospital) for military casualties. Plas Newydd was also considered for use as a hospital during the early part of the war.

The naval training school HMS *Conway*, stationed on the River Mersey, moved to the Menai Straits in 1941. Locals were astonished to see a large wooden ship sailing into the Menai Straits; because of wartime restrictions there was no prior announcement or explanation concerning the move. The ship was moored near Bangor pier. After the war the school was based at Plas Newydd which had been vacated by US Intelligence. In April 1953 she was to famously run aground near the Menai Suspension Bridge where she remained until she was destroyed by fire in 1956.

It was probably inevitable that the evacuation of hundreds of children from English cities would not be without its problems. While the welcome they received was reasonably cordial, there were obviously those who were less than keen on the idea and very soon the local papers were full of complaints. Most frequent was that the allowance given for each child, which varied between 8s 6d and 10s 6d, was insufficient to feed them, let alone provide anything else. There were also frequent complaints that some evacuees had reached their destination in a dirty condition. Others complained that the children came from the lowest strata of society and were frequently troublesome and unruly. There were also those who were against the billeting of evacuees with local families; they felt that the probable social effects of evacuees on rural areas would be alleviated by housing them in camps which would function as self-contained townships. In short, evacuees were not welcomed by everyone.

Of course there were cultural, linguistic and religious differences between most of the evacuees and the people of Anglesey. On 22 September it was reported that there were 780 children and 250 mothers, all Liverpool Catholics, in eight centres in Anglesey. The Revd William Hudson of St Vincent's School, Liverpool, was quoted as saying that the people of Anglesey had been kindness itself towards them. He added that children had been taken to better homes than most had in Liverpool and they had been so fussed over that they were in danger of being spoilt. He also stated that some mothers had come to Anglesey to take their children back (because there were no air raids), but that the children did not wish to return! In 1939, there were just three Catholic churches in Anglesey (Beaumaris, Amlwch and Holyhead); it was reported in late September that Catholic services for evacuees had also been held at Gwalchmai and Aberffraw.

Welsh Nonconformists and Roman Catholics were not always comfortable bedfellows, and this unease surfaced from time to time. The Holyhead Free Church Council met on 15 September to discuss an application by Anglesey Education Committee for use of three Holyhead chapel schoolrooms – Bethphage (Llaingoch), Hebron (both Presbyterian chapels) and Ebeneser (Baptist) – as day schools for evacuees. The meeting agreed to this request but stipulated that 'no teaching of a Roman Catholic nature can be allowed in them'. Nowadays such a request would scarcely raise an eyebrow, but in 1939 a certain religious narrowness sometimes came to the surface. The Holyhead Free Church Council also expressed the concern that more should have been done to ensure that 'all evacuees were healthy and clean'.

The Welsh Presbyterian Chapel of Bryn Du, near Llanfaelog, was used during the week by a Liverpool Catholic school which had been evacuated to the area.

At the beginning of November it was reported that 20 children of the Holy Cross Roman Catholic Elementary School in Liverpool were receiving daily instruction and attending Sunday Mass at St Thomas' (Anglican) Church Hall at Newborough with the Revd Fr Keegan of Colwyn Bay officiating. St Thomas' Church (known locally as Eglwys Bach) is situated near the centre of the village and is now a community centre. A few miles away, the Methodist chapel at Bryn Du (near Llanfaelog) was taken over on weekdays by a Catholic School from Liverpool. The vestry of Llannerch-y-medd Baptist Chapel (Tabernacle) was used as a school for evacuees from West Kirby.

Alsop High School, Liverpool, was evacuated to Holyhead and received their lessons at Holyhead County School. Local pupils were educated between 8.15 a.m. and 1.00 p.m., and the Liverpool pupils in the afternoons. In a local newspaper article, the head boy B. Lake was quoted as saying, 'we have made a thorough revision of our view on the Welsh people, totally in their favour, although we still fail to be convinced of the merits of Lloyd George and Liberalism'. One wonders what his views of the Welsh were before moving to Holyhead!

On Friday 6 October 1939 the Woolworth company opened their 'new super store' in Bangor. Their proud boast was 'nothing over sixpence'. The Woolworth store, much frequented by generations of people from the south-eastern part of Anglesey, remained in its prominent high street location until its closure in January 2009; the 1930s styling is very evident on the upper parts of the building.

In early October there was a 'call-up' into the armed forces for men aged 21 and those who had reached 20 since 3 June 1939. This was a total of 250,000 men. Conscription was initially very unpopular; some of its most vociferous opponents in Wales were Nonconformist Chapel Ministers. Also in October discussions began about the use of allotments for the growing of foodstuffs. The allotment was to prove a useful way of supplementing the nation's food supply during the conflict and growing vegetables in this way became a popular pastime during the war. There were allotments in most of Anglesey's towns.

The 'Phoney War' continued for some months after war was declared. There was no fighting in France and no air raids in Britain. British aircraft continued to fly over Germany but only dropped propaganda leaflets. However, there were losses at sea due to continued activity by German U-boats.

At the time though, there was a great deal of speculation about a possible German invasion of Britain. Although southern and eastern England would probably be the most logical places for this to occur, there were many parts of Britain where it was felt the coastline was vulnerable. In Anglesey, the wide expanse of Red Wharf Bay was considered an ideal location for such an invasion. Trees were felled and placed across all roads and access points and a wire fence ran for miles across the beach. As these proved to be inadequate, huge boulders were placed near the shore where they would block the path of any invaders. However, these were moved by the sea and were rendered ineffective. It was then decided to use long stakes which were placed deep in the sand and these filled the whole beach. There they remained until the end of the hostilities when they were removed by prisoners of war.

Near the breakwater in Holyhead, pillboxes were constructed inside existing structures, such as these Gothic folly towers. Anti-invasion measures took many different forms on the island.

A pillbox near Hermon, overlooking the estuary at Malltraeth.

Some events carried on as usual, although some compromise for wartime conditions was inevitable. The first Menai Bridge Fair (Ffair y Borth) of the war was held on Tuesday 24 October. Not surprisingly, numbers were reported to be down on previous years and no open lights were allowed after dark.

At the end of October it was reported that there were 110 German prisoners being held in Britain and a handful of British prisoners in Germany. The government stated that there was no question of an exchange. In early November there were brief reports of conditions in Nazi concentration camps at Buchenwald and Dachau. The British people would have to wait until 1945 to learn the true horror of these camps.

On 10 November the tragic submarine *Thetis* was dry-docked at Holyhead harbour where the work of removing 34 more bodies was to continue. Fourteen more victims of the tragedy were buried in Holyhead on 16 November. Also on that day, the 'Holyhead War Emergency Committee for the Welfare of Men at the Front and their Dependents' began its work. The intention was to draw up a full list of Holyhead men who were on active service, and to provide financial aid for deserving cases.

In mid-December the National Savings Campaign was launched in North Wales. The campaign encouraged people to be thrifty and to invest in National Savings Certificates, Defence Bonds, National Savings Stamps and other forms of government investment. The intention was, of course, to raise money for the war effort. Two months later, it was announced that these schemes had raised over £60 million. However, in a December meeting of the Holyhead War Savings Committee, a certain Mr R.M. Bell described Holyhead as 'poverty stricken' and claimed that the people of Holyhead had 'little to save'. In fact the people of Holyhead made an exceptional contribution to National Savings throughout the war.

Although a wartime Christmas could hardly be the same as a normal Christmas, many Anglesey people were raising funds to buy presents for the troops. Among them were the Llanddona and Llannerch-y-medd Women's Institutes. Despite the conditions many chapels and churches were holding traditional nativity plays and other Christmas events in the usual way.

Anglesey Education Committee announced in December 1939 that, of approximately 3,500 children who had been evacuated to Anglesey at the beginning of the war, about 1,500 had by now returned home. The reason, of course, was that the air raids that the government had feared did not happen and the residents of the cities believed it was safe for their children to return. It is also true that many mothers who had been evacuated with their children found the rural life of Anglesey very boring. They missed the hustle and bustle of life in cities like Liverpool, with its cinemas and pubs, and longed to be home. Some could not understand why the public houses of Anglesey remained closed on Sundays and why the locals attended places of worship in such large numbers!

CHAPTER TWELVE

1940

On 8 January 1940 ham, bacon, butter and sugar were all rationed. This further tightened the grip on a nation already struggling with hardship and adversity. Every family would become familiar with the ration book. The scope of rationing would be extended further during the year, as well as during 1941 and 1942.

Since the Irish Republic was officially neutral, the port of Holyhead authorities had to be particularly vigilant since spies and others with dubious intent could gain entry to Britain from Ireland. Equally, messages could be sent from Britain to the enemy via the Irish Republic. On 12 January 1940, Catherine Harland, a 22-year-old medical student, pleaded guilty in a special Holyhead Police Court to a breach of the 'Control of Communications Order' (a measure intended to prohibit communications between Britain and the enemy). It seems that she intended to travel to the Irish Republic but a letter addressed to a man in Germany was found in her possession. It was apparently her intention to post it in Ireland. The woman was fined £5 even though the letter 'revealed nothing of consequence'.

Less than a month later, in a separate but related court case in Holyhead, Kathleen Mary Pryke, also aged 22, was fined £10 for having letters addressed to Germany in her possession. It seemed they were addressed to men in Germany that the young woman had met on a walking holiday in 1939. There were to be many such cases before the Holyhead courts during the war years.

The Menai Suspension Bridge (then the only road link to the mainland) was designed by Thomas Telford and completed in 1826. Just before the war, in June 1938, work to reconstruct and strengthen the bridge began. The ironwork was to be completely replaced and only the stonework of the original bridge would remain. The work was undertaken by the Dorman-Long company. When war broke out the work was only partly complete; subsequently work continued day and night. On 11 January 1940, construction worker Richard Jones (aged 35) from Penrhosgarnedd, died after falling off the bridge.

In its 26 January edition, the *Chronicle* noted that National Savings Certificates to the value of £31 million had been sold in only two months. On a lighter note, it reported that a mynah bird had been taught to impersonate Lord Haw-Haw, who was described as the 'well-known wireless comedian'.

The Menai Suspension Bridge during its reconstruction between 1938 and 1940.

On 29 January 1940 in a severe storm, the merchant ship *Gleneden*, carrying iron ore to Britain, was holed on Dutchman Bank (south of Puffin Island). The Moelfre lifeboat attended in appalling conditions; there were no shore lights due to the blackout, lighthouses were dimmed and the lifeboat was not equipped with a radio. Sixty men were taken off the striken ship and were brought ashore at Beaumaris. Forty-nine Asian crew members were given food and drink at Beaumaris Town Hall; the eleven British officers were accommodated in hotels. Most of the ship's cargo was later recovered. Typically, the local press did not report this story at the time, but the *Chronicle* reported it in early March. Even then it was not reported that the *Gleneden* had been holed by an enemy torpedo off Bardsey Island and was attempting to reach Liverpool when the ship's pumps could no longer cope. It was decided to beach the vessel on Dutchman's Bank where she subsequently broke up. Wartime censorship probably meant that the full story could not be told.

On Monday 5 February 1940 a British aircraft (a Saro London flying boat) crashed at Holyhead harbour during bad weather, though happily the 11 occupants survived the crash. The incident was not reported by the local press.

On 20 February the pupils of Alsop High School, Liverpool, who had been evacuated to Holyhead, returned home after five months during which time they used the facilities of Holyhead County School. It was considered safe for them to return because the expected heavy enemy bombing had not materialised. A special train was arranged to transport them home. They expressed their gratitude for the welcome they received. When Liverpool was heavily bombed in May 1941, the Alsop School was evacuated again – this time to Bangor.

The pressure on farmers to grow more food was increasing, in fact so much so that they were encouraged to plough and work the land by night. A poster and newspaper advertisement urging farmers to 'Plough now by day and night' was issued early in 1940. In February special regulations were introduced for the lighting of agricultural tractors by night.

It was reported in February that information was beginning to reach Western Europe that the Nazis had already begun the task of the annihilation of the Jews in Poland. Such news was very patchy and even if the British Government knew more of what was actually happening, the press did not report such matters very frequently.

A happier story was that of Hugh Jones, a Holyhead man serving as an engineer on a ship called the *Doric Star*. The crew of this ship had been held prisoner for 11 weeks on a German prison ship called the *Altmark* in very grim conditions. On 16 February the *Altmark* had been trapped in a fjord in neutral Norwegian waters by the British destroyer *Cossack* and 303 British prisoners were released. Another hero of the *Altmark* was second engineer George King of Llangefni, who was also imprisoned with Hugh Jones. The master of the *Altmark*, Captain Heinrich Dau, was later to explain his inhumanity. The *Chronicle* reported that Dau claimed to have been badly treated as a prisoner in Britain during the First World War. According to the *Chronicle*, he was held at a camp near Beaumaris, but it was reported that of those who recalled him, none spoke well of him. The *Altmark* incident came to be regarded as a sign of Nazi brutality, but the liberation of the prisoners was seen in Britain as a morale-booster during the uncertain period of the 'phoney war'.

On 4 March 1940 a Bristol Blenheim (from RAF Bicester) made an emergency forced landing near a small farm called Tyddyn Rhydderch (see Map 3, p. 107) at the eastern extremity of Aberffraw sand dunes. The crew survived but the incident was not reported in the local press.

On 29 March 1940 the government announced that a metal security thread was to be added to all new £1 notes in order to prevent fraud. It was feared that the Germans might smuggle large quantities of forged banknotes into Britain and destabilise the economy. Also in March, rationing was extended to include meat; only meat to the value of 1s 10d per person per week was permitted, though poultry was not rationed.

In April 1940 it was announced that a pipe was to be laid across the Menai Suspension Bridge (then still being reconstructed) to carry water from Bangor to Menai Bridge. The Menai Bridge area had drawn its water from a small reservoir near to where Ysgol David Hughes stands today. The population of Anglesey had increased rapidly since the beginning of the war (because of the presence of evacuees and military personnel) and that sources of water were proving to be inadequate.

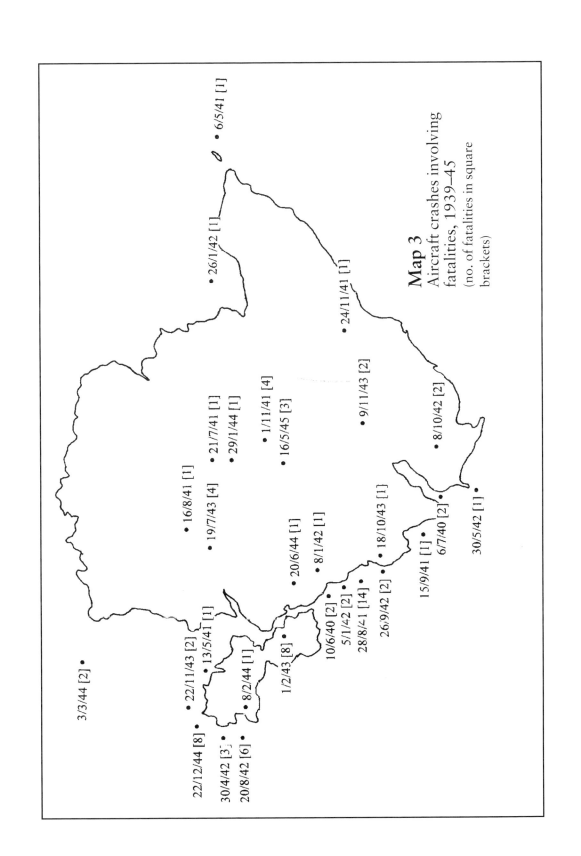

Map 3
Aircraft crashes involving
fatalities, 1939–45
(no. of fatalities in square
brackets)

3/3/44 [2] •

22/11/43 [2] •
13/5/41 [1] •

22/12/44 [8] •
30/4/42 [3] •
20/8/42 [6] •

8/2/44 [1] •

1/2/43 [8] •

10/6/40 [2] •
5/1/42 [2] •
28/8/∠1 [14] •
26/9/42 [2] •

• 16/8/41 [1]

• 19/7/43 [4]

• 20/6/44 [1]
• 8/1/42 [1]

• 18/10/43 [1]

15/9/41 [1] •
6/7/40 [2] •

30/5/42 [1] •

• 21/7/41 [1]
• 29/1/44 [1]

• 1/11/41 [4]
• 16/5/45 [3]

• 9/11/43 [2]

• 8/10/42 [2]

• 26/1/42 [1]

24/11/41 [1] •

• 6/5/41 [1]

Edward Jones of Glasfor, Moelfre, died on 24 April 1940 when the
SS Rydal Force *was sunk by enemy action.*

The coaster SS Rydal Force.

The war at sea was intensifying and there were major losses on both sides. Local papers were increasingly reporting that Anglesey men serving in the Royal Navy and the Merchant Navy had died or were missing. For example, the people of Moelfre were stunned to hear of the deaths of two merchant seamen from the village. They died on 24 April when the coaster *Rydal Force* sank. They were Captain Edward Jones (aged 62) of Glasfor, and his nephew Edwin Owen (aged 25) of Penrhos Terrace. The usual master of the *Rydal Force* was Captain Richard Parry of Benllech; he was lucky to have been home on leave at the time.

In early May 1940, following the withdrawal of British troops from Norway, Neville Chamberlain felt that he had lost the confidence of the nation and even of those in his own party. He resigned and Winston Churchill became Prime Minister of a coalition government (Conservative, Labour and Liberal) that was to run the country for the next five years. Neville Chamberlain remained in the government but died in November 1940.

In May the Holyhead Free Church Council sent a letter to every chapel in the town expressing its concern about the 'moral slackness' that they felt existed in Holyhead. It was claimed that there were houses in Holyhead where 'terrible sins are committed' and that the police were doing their best 'to wipe out these sins'. The Free Church Council claimed that some Holyhead girls and their families were to blame.

On 13 May the SS *Kyle Firth*, carrying crushed stone, ran aground and sank about 2 miles south of South Stack off Penrhos Point (see Map 6, p. 136). This was an accident and not the result of enemy action. The South Stack lighthouse was subject to wartime restrictions and was not illuminated; this made coastal navigation very difficult and dangerous and may have contributed to the accident. The crew of nine were rescued.

On 10 May 1940, Germany invaded the neutral countries of the Netherlands, Belgium and Luxembourg, causing considerable international concern. By the middle of May, the Netherlands had surrendered. Although British and French forces had advanced into Belgium, they failed to stop the advancing Germans. On 15 May Winston Churchill, speaking about the war in the House of Commons, made his famous remark 'I have nothing to offer you but blood, toil, tears and sweat'. It became necessary to evacuate British and Allied forces from Dunkirk between 26 May and 3 June. This was another severe setback.

In May 1940 the ferry ship *Scotia* had been withdrawn from the Holyhead to Dublin route and was used in the Dunkirk evacuation. She was attacked on 1 June by enemy aircraft in the English Channel and a bomb went down the ship's funnel causing massive damage to the engine room. About 2,000 French soldiers aboard were saved but 30 men (mostly in the engine room) were killed. Many of them were from Holyhead. At the end of August 1940, three Holyhead men, William Henry Hughes, R. Parry Williams and James Lewis, were each awarded the Distinguished Service Cross for acts of bravery during this incident. The local press was keen to report acts of bravery, but not so keen to report the loss of life.

On 6 June, Winston Churchill delivered his famous 'we shall fight them on the beaches' speech in the Commons. He also delivered the same speech to the nation on the radio. He reflected the mood and determination of the nation that the Nazis were to be defeated at all costs.

Throughout the rest of 1940 Britain lived in the expectation of a German invasion while the government hastily prepared plans for the country's defence. This is when the Home Guard came into being. On 29 May 1940 the government ordered that all road signs were to be removed. Thus, if the enemy invaded, their progress might be impeded by the lack of direction signs. Railway stations were also stripped of their signs during the war.

On 10 June 1940 a Hawker Henley from RAF Penrhos (on the Llŷn Peninsula) struck the water while flying low in bad weather off Rhosneigr with two fatalities (see Map 3, p. 107). Again, the incident was not reported by the press at the time.

In mid-1940 letters were appearing in the local press expressing concern that Plaid Cymru (always referred to in the *Chronicle* as the 'Welsh Nationalist Party') might be a fifth column, although no evidence to back the claim was offered. At a meeting in Caernarfon in June, Plaid Cymru were demanding 'Dominion Status' for Wales after the war. In the same month a branch of Yr Aelwyd was established in Llangefni. These were clubs established by the Urdd (Welsh League of Youth) for youngsters aged between 14 and 20. This branch at Llangefni was the first in Anglesey and there young people could take part in cycling, swimming, hiking and boxing.

In the middle of June 1940, Italy entered the war and in the same month the British people were shocked and devastated to hear that France had surrendered to Germany. This caused the utmost concern because the enemy was now only a short sea crossing from the south of England. The 'Free French' under General Charles de Gaulle continued their struggle from Britain.

At the end of June the Holyhead Auxiliary Fire Brigade was appealing to men aged 30–50 who were not engaged in other ARP work for assistance. As the war progressed suitable manpower was becoming scarce. There were also discussions at this time to ensure that Anglesey schools were better protected against air raids.

On 30 June the Germans landed on the island of Guernsey and began their occupation of the Channel Islands. This was the only British territory which came under German control during the conflict but it further fuelled fears that a German invasion of mainland Britain was imminent. The Channel Islands remained under German control until 1945; the British Government felt that mounting an invasion to drive out the Germans would only endanger civilians.

On 6 July 1940 a Hawker Henley crashed at sea near Malltraeth with 2 fatalities (see Map 3, p. 107). On 22 July 1940 a 290-ton Admiralty Patrol Boat known as the *Campina* struck a German parachute mine and sank beyond the breakwater at Holyhead. Eleven members of the crew died. The *Campina* was a fishing trawler which had been converted into a patrol vessel in September 1939. On 16 August the 1,598-ton *Lady Meath* (built in 1929) which was carrying large numbers of cattle and sheep was blown up by a mine in the outer harbour; the crew were rescued. The patrol boat *Manx Lad* (originally a fishing vessel hired from an Isle of Man company) went to help the *Lady Meath* but also struck a mine. Luckily no lives were lost.

At the beginning of July the press reported concerns that the Germans were using delayed-action bombs. The public were warned to keep clear of bombs and crashed aircraft.

In July 1940 the Luftwaffe began the bombing attacks which led to the events that became known as the Battle of Britain. The German air force was attempting to control the air over the south of England in order to mount an invasion of Britain. In autumn 1940 the first heavy air raids on British cities began, causing great damage and loss of life. Fortunately, however, British industry was not greatly crippled. The first British raids on Berlin began at about the same time. The Battle of Britain ended in October 1940; the RAF having prevented German domination of the air.

It was reported in July that the Holyhead branch of the National Savings Movement had collected over £52,000 from the sale of Defence Bonds and National Savings Certificates in the first six months of 1940. At the end of July a shop was established in Stanley Street in Holyhead for the sale of National Savings products. The total raised in the War Savings campaign (National Savings Certificates and Defence Bonds) throughout Britain was reported to be £250 million.

At the end of July the government announced plans to call up more men – those born in 1906 and those born between 23 June and 27 July 1920. In early August it was announced that servicemen would receive a pay rise of 6*d* a day. Army pay for the lower ranks at this time was typically just 2*s* per day.

In July rationing was extended to include tea, margarine, cooking fats and cheese. It was also announced that bananas and other fresh or canned fruit were no longer to be imported. Also in July the government interned about 30,000 people considered to be a threat to national security. Many of these people would have been Germans, Austrians or Italians, the majority of whom were interned on the Isle of Man. By the summer of 1941, however, most of them had been released and fewer than 5,000 were still held.

On 22 August a 1,689-ton merchant steamer named the *Thorold* was sunk by German aircraft off the Skerries. The ship was bombed and subjected to gunfire, and during the attack crew members were killed.

At the beginning of September 1940 Anglesey's Police Committee was being urged to appoint women to the ranks of the police force. We should remember that at this time Anglesey had its own police force, before the creation of the Gwynedd force and later the North Wales force. The decision was deferred for three months, but at the end of the year the appointment of policewomen was confirmed. It was announced that three of them would work in Holyhead.

Local fundraising in Anglesey (in common with other areas) included the commencement of a fund to buy a Spitfire (the Ynys Môn Spitfire Fund). By the end of 1940, the fund stood at £688; a list of contributors would appear regularly in the local papers.

During the war the local press made frequent references to conscientious objectors. Most of them felt they could not fight for political, moral or religious reasons and could apply to be placed on a register of Conscientious Objectors. They would then have to appear before tribunals to plead their case. A North Wales Conscientious Objectors Tribunal met from time to time and the proceedings would always be reported in the local press. If exemption from war service was granted, they were allotted work in hospitals, in Civil Defence or on the land. The proportion of those liable for war service who claimed to be conscientious objectors was always very small and declined markedly during the course of the war. Such men were never popular with the public; they were frequently referred to disdainfully as 'Conchies'.

Late on Saturday afternoon 5 October 1940 the first bombs of the war were dropped on the town of Holyhead (see Map 4, p. 113). There were huge explosions followed by anti-aircraft fire. A bomb destroyed a building known as Church House in Boston Street and there was less severe damage to dozens of houses. There were no fatalities. A dance was scheduled to be held in Church House some three hours later; the outcome could therefore have been very different. This was the first of some eleven attacks on Holyhead during the war, nine involving bombing and two involving machine-gunning from aircraft. Fortunately none of these incidents caused any deaths, but there were some injuries.

The 5 October incident was not reported in the press at the time, but it was reported in the *Chronicle* some time later but without specifying the location. This was quite

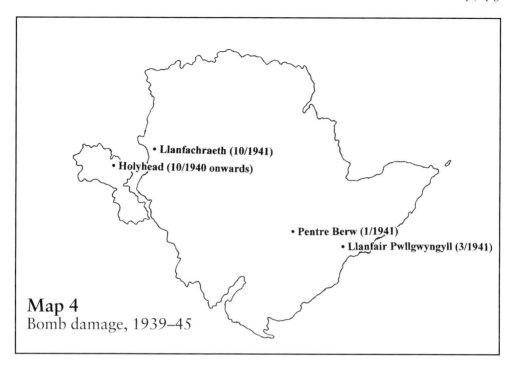

Map 4
Bomb damage, 1939–45

Labels on map:
- Llanfachraeth (10/1941)
- Holyhead (10/1940 onwards)
- Pentre Berw (1/1941)
- Llanfair Pwllgwyngyll (3/1941)

common practice in the papers of the period; incidents such as this would very occasionally be reported but the exact location would not be revealed. Phrases such as 'at a north-west Wales coastal town' or 'North Wales market town' would be used. The inhabitants of Anglesey would, of course, hear about these incidents by word of mouth. The papers would be less likely to report bombing incidents involving loss of life, the reasons being censorship and keeping up the morale of the people. There was also the fear that newspapers, or the information contained in them, might somehow reach enemy hands and that they might discover how successful their raids had been. It is not recorded how many readers the *Chronicle* or *Y Clorianydd* might have had in Nazi Germany, but no chances were being taken.

On 12 October, three German airmen were rescued after their Dornier aircraft was shot down off Carmel Head. An enterprising Holyhead woman volunteered to wash and dry their uniforms and, having done so, placed them on display, charging a small fee. Such was the interest in Nazi uniforms that the sum of 19*s* was raised for the Spitfire Fund!

On 8 November 1940 the sound of a German aircraft was heard over Holyhead. It dropped four bombs, one of which caused damage in Bryn Goleu Avenue (see Map 4, above). A large unexploded bomb was taken to a rifle range at Penrhosfeilw (south of Holyhead) for disposal. The German aircraft apparently crashed near Porth Dafarch, killing the crew.

On 12 November the SS *Eaglescliffe Hall* ran aground in bad weather about half a mile north of Llanddwyn island (see Map 6, p. 136). All the crew survived. A few days later the ship was floated away undamaged on a high tide.

At about this time local papers began carrying advertisements called 'Food Facts' placed by the Ministry of Food (which had been established in 1937, in anticipation of a possible war), urging people not to be wasteful with food, suggesting recipes and giving useful tips. One such advertisement in late November 1940 included details of how to make an oven out of an old biscuit tin. A paragraph in the *Chronicle* urged people to collect nuts from the hedgerows. It stated, rather inappropriately, that 'English nuts may be had for the picking on a weekend ramble along country lanes'. The item, probably copied from another newspaper or publication, made no reference to Welsh nuts. Unlike today, Britain was frequently referred to as 'England' at that time.

On 6 December the SS *Watkin F. Nesbitt* drifted ashore in a gale just north of the Llanddwyn island lighthouse (see Map 6, p. 136), resulting in one fatality. It proved impossible to salvage the whole ship and therefore the vessel was cut in half with the aft section being floated away so that the engine room could be salvaged.

A 'War Weapons Week' was held at Holyhead in early December 1940 and was opened by Megan Lloyd George (Anglesey's Liberal MP and the daughter of David Lloyd George). The target was £40,000. However, an astonishing £90,261 was raised. This amount, equivalent to several millions today, was raised in a town previously described as 'poverty stricken'. Apparently, the people of Holyhead saw themselves as being in competition with Conwy (with a similar population), but Holyhead raised the larger sum by far.

As if the war wasn't enough to burden the poor people of Anglesey, an earth tremor shook much of Anglesey and Caernarfonshire on 12 December. It was centred on the Llŷn Peninsula and measured 4.7 on the Richter Scale. In British terms, this would be regarded as a substantial tremor. During wartime conditions with the fear of enemy bombing and poorer communications, it caused some considerable panic with reports of people running into the streets.

In December the shops of Anglesey and Bangor were keenly advertising their Christmas wares in the local papers. Although wartime restrictions had a profound effect, it seems that a surprising amount of Christmas fare was on offer, including beers, wines and spirits. Ration coupons, though, would have been necessary to buy a lot of them.

Work began in 1940 on the RAF airfield at Valley (see Map 5, p. 125). The RAF needed a large number of airfields in order to secure sufficient air cover in all parts of the United Kingdom, and it was felt that areas in the west were inadequately covered. Attacks had not been expected from that direction but German aircraft had approached from the west and attacked targets on Merseyside. The most mountainous areas of North Wales were obviously unsuitable for airfields, but Anglesey, being largely flat, was seen as an ideal location. The process of building the airfield began with the levelling of the sand dunes at Tywyn Trewan.

The site of Bodorgan airfield with some remaining wartime buildings.

RAF Bodorgan tried to requisition this nearby Presbyterian Chapel (Capel Beulah) for their own use during the war, but were unsuccessful.

Work also began in 1940 on Anglesey's smallest airfield at Bodorgan (see Map 5, p. 125). Land south of the village of Hermon was requisitioned. This land was part of the Bodorgan Estate (owned by Sir George Meyrick of Bodorgan Hall). The airfield opened on 1 November 1940 and was initially called RAF Aberffraw. The airfield itself was extremely basic, merely a grass field without the usual tarmac runways and because of the nature of the set-up here, it often became flooded and unusable in winter. There were a few hangars and other buildings on the site. It is interesting to note that the RAF tried to requisition a nearby Presbyterian chapel known as Capel Beulah for their own use, but there were objections and their attempt was unsuccessful.

The aircraft flown from Bodorgan were known as Queen Bees; these were pilotless, radio-controlled versions of the De Havilland Tiger Moth trainer aircraft. They were used for gunnery practice for soldiers in the Tŷ Croes anti-aircraft artillery range. Bodorgan was often used for aircraft storage; there were at various times up to 30 large

Some remaining Second World War buildings on the site of the former RAF Bodorgan.

aircraft on the site. Although it would have been an easy target, the site was never attacked by the enemy. In May 1941 the name of the airfield was changed to RAF Bodorgan; apparently some people could not pronounce 'Aberffraw'!

CHAPTER THIRTEEN

1941

The new year started with some good news for the people of Anglesey and all those who regularly crossed to and from the island. The reconstruction of the Menai Suspension Bridge was complete and on 1 January 1941 the toll to cross the bridge was abolished. There had been a toll on the bridge since it was built in 1826. During the war the bridge (as well as the Britannia railway bridge) was routinely guarded by uniformed men and police, in case of saboteurs. The movement of vessels through the straits was strictly controlled and the area was patrolled by boats based at Fort Belan (near Dinas Dinlle, Caernarfonshire). Permission was needed by any vessel wishing to pass under the bridges and there were also secret contingency plans concerning the action that could be taken should either or both bridges be rendered unusable by enemy action.

In January 1941 explosives (parachute mines) were dropped on Pentre Berw (see Map 4, p. 113). There was damage to some houses, some greenhouses and the roof of Pen-y-Sarn Methodist Chapel was badly damaged, but there were no deaths. It

The Presbyterian Chapel of Pen-y-Sarn, Pentre Berw, was badly damaged by bombing in January 1941.

was believed that the greenhouses had been visible from the air and this may have prompted the attack. Alternatively, the crew could simply have been getting rid of surplus bombs; this was a common practice for crews returning to their bases.

With the war in full swing Anglesey found itself having to cope with very large numbers of people from outside Wales – evacuees, soldiers and airmen. There were complaints, sometimes expressed in letters to the press, that these incomers had not the slightest idea how to pronounce Welsh names. One such letter, from Margaret Evans of Menai Bridge, complained 'they regard their persistent mispronunciations as humorous rather than discourteous'.

Early in 1941 the Bodorgan airfield was expanded by 15 acres (situated between Bodorgan Hall and the existing airfield) to accommodate what was referred to as a satellite landing ground. This was essentially a storage space for aircraft for the RAF Maintenance Unit at RAF Hawarden in north-east Wales. The airfield was used for a number of aircraft, including Hurricanes and the larger Wellingtons. Landing a Wellington at Bodorgan would have required considerable flying skills because of the distinct lack of space and the strong cross-winds.

The railways played an important role in the war effort. The rail network was much larger then – Anglesey had three lines, only one of which (Llanfair Pwllgwyngyll to Holyhead) is still in use today. The LMS were keen to see more women employed in various capacities (porters and clerical workers, for example) on the railways, but the employment of women on the railways became a controversial subject in Holyhead with protests from the National Union of Railwaymen. The debate continued for some time.

As mentioned already, the port of Holyhead was always vigilant in case spies and other suspicious characters passed through, to and from the Irish Republic. Staff were stationed there to keep a close eye on any shady individuals. There were fairly frequent cases throughout the war years of Irishmen passing through Holyhead and carrying papers falsely representing themselves as members of His Majesty's forces. Whatever the reasons for their deceit (and such information was rarely reported even if it was known to the authorities) the perpetrators were severely punished and usually given prison sentences.

In February 1941 it was reported that an Anglesey garage proprietor was fined £10 after being found guilty of supplying petrol mixed with the cheaper paraffin. In times of shortage such cases were frequent. The following month some Holyhead butchers were fined for supplying sausages which did not meet wartime regulations, and an Anglesey farmer was fined for adding water to milk. There were to be many such cases throughout the war. There were always people willing to flout the rules for their own gain.

There was an enormous explosion during a night raid by German bombers on Holyhead on 25 February 1941 (see Map 4, p. 113). Damage was caused to the Harbourmaster's House on Salt Island, but three streets – Front Bath Street, Back Bath Street and Parliament Ditch – were wrecked beyond hope of repair. There was less severe damage in other parts of the town. Fortunately, once again, there were no deaths.

On 3 March 1941 the first squadrons of aircraft arrived at the newly constructed RAF Valley airfield. It had three runways but the site was in a bleak and exposed location with very little in the way of comforts for the staff – it was initially envisaged that it would have only a short life. At the beginning, the airfield was known as RAF Rhosneigr, but this was changed on 5 April to RAF Valley, probably because 'Valley' was easier to pronounce!

Valley became home to a large number of different squadrons and units at different times, including Belgian, Polish and Czech pilots. It would later be used by the US Air Force. Sadly, RAF Valley would not be without its problems: the airfield was close to an extensive area of sand dunes and sand entering aircraft engines was a constant (and very expensive) problem. The airfield also had a poor safety record; there were many accidents in its 4½-year wartime history. A nearby chapel hall (belonging to Caergeiliog Presbyterian Chapel) was also used for a time as an operations room by RAF Valley.

On 12 March 1941, a number of bombs fell at Llanfair Pwllgwyngyll, including one on the Gors field, one south of the village near a house called Llwyn Onn and one at Maenafon Terrace in Ffordd Penmynydd (see Map 4, p. 113). In fact 8 Maenafon Terrace was virtually demolished and one other house badly damaged. There were no deaths. Two days later, two bombs fell near Plas Newydd.

Maenafon Terrace, Llanfair Pwllgwyngyll, was bombed in March 1941. No. 8 was badly damaged.

Gwalia Stores, Beaumaris, was badly damaged by a Spitfire on 13 March 1941.

On 13 March 1941 a Supermarine Spitfire from RAF Hawarden being flown by a Canadian pilot developed a fault. The pilot bailed out and landed unhurt near Gallows Point, just outside Beaumaris, while his aircraft continued its descent and crashed into the middle of the town. Astonishingly perhaps, no-one was killed but a shop known as Gwalia Stores and an adjoining house at the junction of New Street and Rose Hill were very badly damaged by the crash and the subsequent fire. One of the occupiers of these properties was taken to hospital and both of these properties were later repaired. In fact Gwalia Stores continued in business until 2009.

It was reported in mid-March that the Holyhead Free Church Council was opposing the showing of films in cinemas on Sundays. It seems that Holyhead Council intended sanctioning cinema and entertainment on Sundays for Dutch visitors to the town. This gave rise to a furious debate; Welsh Nonconformist leaders believed that Sunday was to be left alone and they did not take kindly to any attempt to reverse this.

In March rationing was extended to marmalade, jam, treacle and syrup. In the same month the Ministry of Supply were advertising in the local press for binoculars; the advertisement stated that the ministry was prepared to pay for them or accept them as gifts.

On the night of 9 April 1941 a bomb was dropped within 200 yards of Church House in Holyhead (which had been destroyed by bombing in October 1940). This

The Wesleyan Methodist Chapel of Bethel Glan y Môr, Holyhead, was damaged by bombing in April 1941.

caused damage to Bethel Wesleyan Chapel, a garage, surrounding buildings and railway sidings across the road (see Map 4, p. 113). Dozens of houses were slightly damaged but there were no fatalities. Other bombs and incendiaries were dropped during this raid in the harbour area; fortunately they missed an ammunition train loaded with cargo from a Canadian ship. Had the bombs hit the ship or the train, the devastation would have been on a massive scale. Large quantities of explosives were often unloaded at Holyhead because the port of Liverpool had been crippled by enemy bombing.

The War Weapons Week held at Holyhead in December 1940 was extended to the rest of Anglesey and was held in the week of 19–26 April 1941. The target was set at £250,000 including the £90,000 previously raised in Holyhead. The week involved various activities and parades; in Beaumaris, a procession involved the Royal Marines, the Home Guard and the clergy. The final total for Anglesey (including Holyhead) was £573,695 which worked out as a staggering £11.20 per person! We have to remember that this was 1941 Anglesey, a depressed area where the average weekly wage would have been less than £5.

On 6 May, a Blackburn Botha crashed in the sea near Puffin Island with one fatality. The incident went unreported. Between 6 and 9 May, Holyhead was attacked three times (with high explosive bombs, parachute mines and machine-gun fire). On the third of these occasions, the German aircraft was brought down in the sea.

On 10 May one of the most bizarre incidents of the war took place. Rudolf Hess, Adolf Hitler's deputy, flew a light aircraft and landed in Scotland. It was believed that he might be trying to arrange a peace deal. But whatever the purpose of his mission, no peace deal materialised and Hess spent the rest of the war in prison.

Evacuees were the source of considerable debate throughout the year. In Valley it was reported in May that evacuees were behaving in a rowdy manner outside places of worship. The local council suggested that the Liverpool authorities be asked to send a priest and welfare workers to keep them under control. It was also claimed that a group of recently arrived evacuees had been virtually impossible to billet owing to their dirty condition. For various reasons some householders would occasionally refuse to accept evacuees, even though such people could be fined for ignoring a compulsory billeting order. Later in the year Holyhead Council actually paid compensation to three householders for damage caused by evacuees. There were also complaints in letters to the press that small homes without spare rooms tended to get evacuees billeted on them whereas large houses 'mysteriously keep their peacetime conditions'. These were further examples of the friction that could be generated by the uneasy relationship between evacuees and locals.

In June rationing was extended to eggs and their distribution came to be controlled by the Ministry of Food. Each person was allowed only one fresh egg per week. The meat ration had been cut several times since its introduction in March and now stood at 1s per person per week. On 6 July, bus services were curtailed by 50 per cent on Sundays in order to conserve fuel. In a rural area like Anglesey with few people sufficiently privileged to own a car, this would have been a considerable inconvenience.

Among the more innovative means of raising funds for the war was a 'mile of pennies'. In Holyhead on 12 July £43 9s 3d was raised for the Merchant Service Fund. Not as effective as the War Weapons Week perhaps, but all contributions were welcome.

On 21 July, a Boulton Paul Defiant from RAF Valley crashed near Llannerch-y-medd (see Map 3, p. 107) and the pilot was killed. Three days later bombs were dropped near Aberffraw; no damage was reported but some sheep were killed.

The National Eisteddfod was held at Colwyn Bay in the first week of August and although it was good to keep up some semblance of normality in wartime, the event was curtailed to a three-day event. A 27-year-old Llangefni solicitor, Rolant H. Jones (known also as Rolant o Fôn), won the Eisteddfod Chair.

In August a War Prisoners Adoption Scheme was announced whereby members of the public could 'adopt' a British prisoner of war and send him a parcel containing some useful commodities. Sending each parcel would cost 10s – a considerable sum of money in 1941.

On 23 August Holyhead was the scene of a large-scale 'mock invasion'. This was a major exercise involving the Navy, the Army and the RAF as well as Civil Defence services such as the Fire Brigade, the Auxiliary Fire Service, the Ambulance Service and the police. Planes dive-bombed the town and dropped smoke bombs. Tear gas was also used. 'Fifth columnists' guided 'invaders' and 'saboteurs' to various locations. The public were urged to carry their gas masks.

On the morning of Thursday 28 August 1941 during very severe late summer weather, an RAF twin-engined Blackburn Botha with a three-man crew based at Valley came down immediately after take-off in the sea off Traeth Crigyll, Rhosneigr (see Map 3, p. 107). Ordinarily an aircraft would never have flown in such weather, but a report had been received that a convoy was being attacked by U-boats and action had to be taken. A rescue by local villagers, RAF Valley personnel, soldiers from the Tŷ Croes Camp, a local policeman and others was launched. Three men could be seen clinging to the plane which was in shallow water. Rescuers used a boat but it was swamped by the strong wind and swell. Another boat was launched to rescue the rescuers, but their efforts were in vain as 14 people lost their lives, including the three who were on the aircraft. The rescue efforts were seen by hundreds of onlookers, both locals and holidaymakers. The soldiers who died (from a Royal Artillery Regiment) were buried in nearby Llanfaelog churchyard. The five military graves are in the newer part of the cemetery. Three local men were among the dead, Evan Jones (aged 39, a Coastguard, buried at Rhoscolyn), Arthur J. Owen (a Merchant Navy Second Officer who was home on leave) and PC George Cledwyn Arthur (aged 29 and a native of Amlwch).

Traeth Crigyll, Rhosneigr. This was the scene of an aircraft disaster involving a Blackburn Botha, the rescue efforts of which turned out to be a tragedy, 28 August 1941.

A plaque near the fire station at Rhosneigr dedicated to the memory of the men who died in the aircraft disaster in August 1941.

The *Chronicle* did not report the incident until 3 October, but a fuller account was not given until 31 October following an inquest at Rhosneigr. Two of the rescuers who survived, Stewart Wood and Derrick Hubert Baynham (both aged 17 and on holiday in the area), received the George Medal from King George VI on 28 April 1942. They also received the RNLI silver medal for gallantry and silver cigarette cases from General Władysław Sikorski, the Commander-in-Chief of the Polish forces. This was because the aircraft's pilot (Sergeant Kazimierz Stefan Rosiewicz, aged 23) was Polish. His body was not washed ashore until 11 September, after which he was buried at St Mary's Catholic Cemetery at Holyhead. Four other rescuers, Sergeant C. Jackson, Lance Bombadier T. Taylor, Gunner J.W. Parkinson and Aircraftsman Albert E. Atkinson were awarded bronze medals.

It is interesting to note that Derrick Baynham joined the Army in 1942 where he remained after the war. He retired in 1979 having reached the rank of Brigadier; he died in May 2006 aged 82. PC George Arthur was posthumously awarded the King's Commendation for Brave Conduct in January 1942. There is a memorial to this tragedy in Rhosneigr. It was erected in 1991, largely through the efforts of Arthur Jones, the son of Evan Jones, the Coastguard.

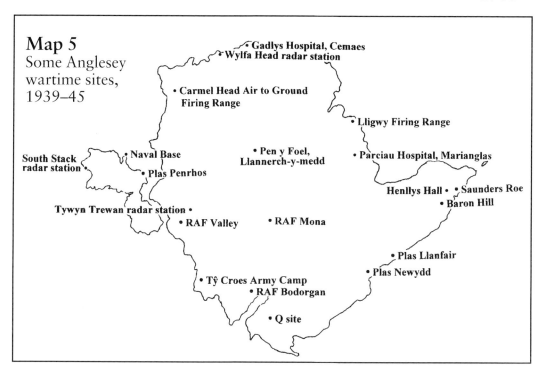

Map 5
Some Anglesey
wartime sites,
1939–45

Gadlys Hospital, Cemaes
Wylfa Head radar station

• Carmel Head Air to Ground
Firing Range

• Lligwy Firing Range

South Stack
radar station

• Naval Base

• Plas Penrhos

• Pen y Foel,
Llannerch-y-medd

• Parciau Hospital, Marianglas

Henllys Hall • • Saunders Roe
• Baron Hill

Tywyn Trewan radar station •

• RAF Valley

• RAF Mona

• Plas Llanfair

• Plas Newydd

• Tŷ Croes Army Camp
• RAF Bodorgan

• Q site

Towards the end of 1941, activity at RAF Valley had increased considerably and it was felt that it should be protected by the building of a decoy site – this was common practice for busy airfields. The large area of sand dunes near Newborough (about 8 miles away) was the chosen location (see Map 5, above) and construction began in November 1941. This site (known as a Q-site) was operated at night and took the form of Drem landing lights which were intended to trick the enemy into thinking they were flying over Valley. The Drem lighting system had been developed at RAF Drem in East Lothian in 1940 and it became the standard system at all RAF airfields. The Newborough Q-site was operated by a small team of men under the direction of RAF Valley. If German aircraft bombed the site, only the sand dunes would be damaged. The site failed to attract any enemy interest, but was the scene of a tragedy involving an Allied aircraft in 1942 (see Chapter 14).

On 15 September 1941 a Bristol Blenheim ran out of fuel and was abandoned by its crew near Bodorgan (see Map 3, p. 107). Two survived but one drowned. Also in September Holyhead Council decided to establish a 'British Restaurant' in the town. They decided to requisition the Railway Institute Building for conversion for the purpose. British Restaurants were essentially communal kitchens which were set up by the Ministry of Food and they were to be found in most large towns. Run by local committees and run on a non-profit-making basis, most of these establishments were very spartan and resembled works canteens but they were open to anyone and no ration coupons were needed to use them. They proved popular during the war as a main meal would cost only 1s 6d.

In October the *Chronicle* reported a most peculiar story concerning the discovery of a semi-conscious man in a wooden crate in Dublin. It seems the crate had been shipped from Holyhead and when opened in Dublin, was found to contain a Frenchman. The man, aged about 40, was described as a well-known French painter and former member of the French Air Force. No further details were reported.

On 16 October a mobile canteen was presented to the council at Holyhead. Such canteens were used to feed the homeless and rescuers in the event of severe damage caused by an air raid. It was to be run by the WVS, but Holyhead Town Council had the responsibility of maintaining it in good order.

On 24 October some houses in Llanfachraeth were damaged by enemy action, but there were no injuries.

Breaches of the Control of Communications order were still being detected in Holyhead. In late October 1941, an Irish Roman Catholic priest named Joseph E. Brown was fined £5 for carrying letters through the port in contravention of the order.

On Saturday 1 November 1941 a German Heinkel bomber was shot down over Anglesey by an Australian pilot stationed at RAF Valley. Wreckage was spread over a wide area but most of the aircraft landed in a field not far from the village of Bodffordd (see Map 3, p. 107). The aircraft burst into flames and its cargo of bombs exploded causing damage to two houses and considerable distress to their occupants. All four of the German crew died. No trace of the pilot was ever found; the German Volksbund database claims he fell into the sea. The bodies of the other three crew members were buried at Holyhead. Some years later they were exhumed and reinterred at Cannock Chase German Cemetery. This incident was not reported in the press, although the demise of an enemy aircraft might have been thought of as a morale-booster. On the other hand, the presence of enemy aircraft in Anglesey's airspace might have caused worry. This crash proved to be something of a novelty – news of the incident spread quickly and crowds of onlookers gathered to survey the wreckage.

On 24 November 1941 two Supermarine Spitfires collided in mid-air near Llanfair Pwllgwyngyll (see Map 3, p. 107); one pilot died, the other survived.

At the beginning of December it was reported that the LMS *Cambria*, sailing between Holyhead and Ireland, had been attacked by enemy torpedoes. However, the attack was unsuccessful and the ship (with 200 passengers) was undamaged. This showed clearly that German aircraft and U-boats were active in the Irish Sea.

On 8 December the government introduced a scheme known as the 'Vitamin Welfare Scheme'. All children under the age of two received free supplies of cod liver oil, blackcurrant juice and orange juice (when it was available). This was in response to concerns that the wartime diet was inadequate for very young children. The provision of free school milk also began around this time, each pupil being supplied with milk in the familiar $1/3$-pint bottles. State schools also began providing midday meals. Milk rationing began in December 1941 with each person being allowed 3 pints per week.

Holyhead's Maritime Museum was previously a lifboat hut. It was used by the Royal Dutch Merchant Marines during the Second World War.

In exceptional cases, such as expectant mothers, more would be allowed. National dried milk was introduced at the same time.

The Second World War saw a substantial increase in crime. Anglesey was no exception and the courts were kept busy. The constant movement of population and the fact that there were a lot of new people in the community was undoubtedly a factor in this. Separate court cases in December 1941 involved a Dutch woman with a husband in the Dutch navy (fined £5 for stealing two £1 notes), an Australian in the RAF (acquitted of stealing a vase), and an 11-year-old boy evacuated to Holyhead appeared in court on charges of theft. The boy stole a bar of soap valued at 6d from Tŷ Croes railway station. He was bound over for two years in the sum of £5 and had to be indoors at 6.30 p.m. every day. Harsh treatment perhaps, but the increasing level of petty crime (including juvenile crime) was causing concern and the punishment had to act as a deterrent to others.

The year ended with the usual Christmas celebrations and Nativity plays. In Dwyran, it was reported that the evacuees of the Webster Road School, Liverpool, gave a concert and performed English and Welsh items for their 'foster parents'. At the end of the second complete year of the war, the government announced that Boxing Day 1941 would not be a holiday. It was felt that the loss of war production would be detrimental.

CHAPTER FOURTEEN

1942

In 1942 newspapers carried advertisements proclaiming that 10,000 women from North Wales were needed to give vital aid for the armed forces of Britain and Russia (on the side of the Allies since mid-1941). 5,000 were needed for the ATS and 5,000 for war factories in North Wales. This was open to women aged 18–60 and offered a basic pay of between £2 5s and £2 9s a week.

A letter from the RSPCA in the local press in January 1942 informed the public that cats were being stolen for their fur, so owners were being urged to keep their cats indoors at night. Another letter urged the collection of salvage (tins, paper and so on) from rural areas in Anglesey. It seems the practice (which we would now call recycling) was common in the urban areas, but not in the rural parts of the island.

On 5 January 1942 a Bristol Beaufighter (from Valley) crashed at Rhosneigr, resulting in the death of two crewmen (see Map 3, p. 107). On 8 January a Supermarine Spitfire and a Westland Lysander were involved in a mid-air collision near RAF Valley. The Polish pilot of the Lysander was killed and he was later buried at Llangadwaladr cemetery. On 26 January a Hawker Sea Hurricane came down in the sea off Red Wharf Bay. The pilot escaped from the aircraft but sadly drowned. None of these incidents was reported in the local press.

On 7 February soap rationing began with each person being allowed one small tablet per month. Washing powder was also rationed. The rationing of soap was to last until 1950.

Following the phenomenal success of the War Weapons Week in Anglesey in 1941, it was decided to hold a Warship Week between 21 and 28 February. The target was £637,000 for the purchase of a Hunt Class Destroyer (£500,000) and a minesweeper to be named *Beaumaris* (£137,000). As before, each area was allocated a target figure. The events in the Warship Week included processions, street collections, a ball, football matches, dances, whist drives, boxing matches and various types of entertainment including a cinema van. The final figures for the Warship Week showed that the island had fallen well short of its target. This was the only time during the war that an Anglesey fundraising campaign failed to reach its target. All the island's towns and rural areas had failed to reach their individual targets and the total raised was £332,900. The figures were quoted in the *Chronicle* without comment and it was April before a local councillor was reported as suggesting that the failure of the Warship Week to reach its targets was due to the losses and reverses experienced by British forces in the Far East and the Middle East. Perhaps the target was also unrealistically high bearing in mind the Warship Week campaign came only ten months after the War Weapons Week.

Another example of wartime lawbreaking was evident at Holyhead in March 1942 when several employees of the LMS railway company were charged with theft. Most of those found guilty were fined, but one local man was jailed for two months.

The government was now actively discouraging unnecessary travel, especially by car. It was also announced that no extra trains and buses would be provided over Easter.

At the end of March the Anglesey Education Committee stated that there were 1,382 evacuees receiving their education in Anglesey, with 926 being educated by Liverpool teachers in special premises. It was reported that of 256 teachers employed by the authority, 179 were women. Of 56 Liverpool teachers, only 7 were men.

In April the Chancellor of the Exchequer Sir Kingsley Wood delivered his budget and increased the price of beer and tobacco to twice their pre-war levels. Purchase tax was doubled (from 33.3 to 66.6 per cent) on luxury items (silk, fur coats and so on). However, there were income tax concessions for those on low incomes.

In April the Clerk of Holyhead Council stated that all railings and gates, including those belonging to chapels and churches were to be removed and used for salvage. There were further discussions and much opposition over the next few weeks; perhaps unsurprisingly the Holyhead Free Church Council was very much opposed to removing railings from places of worship.

At this point in the war there had been a huge increase in the number of young women in the Women's Land Army. In North Wales, there were 60 women in the Land

Gwanwyn Jones of Menai Bridge did her bit for the war effort by working as a 'lumberjill'.

Army in 1941, but this had risen to 400 in 1942. On 27 April, a hostel was opened for the Women's Land Army in Holyhead Road, Menai Bridge (on part of a tennis court near to the present-day telephone exchange). The hostel was a wooden building which contained a kitchen, recreation room and sleeping quarters; the accommodation was considered fairly basic. Most of the Land Girls were reported to be from Lancashire, a few from North Wales and one from Holland. Land Army hostels were later built at Valley (near the location of the Tan-y-Bryn estate) and at Llannerch-y-medd.

At the beginning of May, the press reported that clothes donated by the USA, Canada, Australia and New Zealand were stored in the County Depot in Church Street, Llangefni. These garments were for the use of people who were bombed out of their homes and were sorted into clothes for men, women, boys and girls. There were sub-depots in various other parts of the island.

In May it was claimed that the tide of war was turning in favour of the Allies. Nevertheless, in the same month the Prime Minister, Winston Churchill, warned the British people about the possible use of poison gas by the Germans. He reminded them to check their gas masks and to know always where they were.

There were discussions concerning milk supply to the island at this time and it was reported in May 1942 that some in the agricultural industry favoured the establishment of a milk factory in Anglesey.

On 30 May 1942 a Blackburn Botha came down near Llanddwyn Island. The pilot survived, but a passenger drowned.

The basic petrol ration ceased on 1 June 1942 and petrol for private motoring was no longer available. In practice this meant that most motorists were unable to use their cars and that only essential car use (e.g. by doctors and other key workers) was permitted. The *Chronicle* gave its readers tips on how to store car batteries for a prolonged period.

Dried egg powder (imported from the USA as a result of the Lend-Lease agreement of 1941) became available in tins or packets for the first time in June and became a familiar food during the war. It was not popular with housewives as it was difficult to use. It was during this period that horsemeat also became available. In July rationing was extended to sweets. The government felt that sugar could be put to better use, and many familiar favourites all but disappeared from the shelves for the remainder of the war and beyond.

At the end of June in a court case at Holyhead, a Llaingoch man (who worked as a fireman on a mail boat) was found guilty of smuggling various items into Holyhead including, sugar, butter, chocolate, sausages, bacon and whisky. He was fined £15. The authorities took these cases very seriously and substantial fines were usually imposed.

On 20 August 1942 a Vickers Wellington (from RAF Dale) came down in the sea off South Stack (see Map 3, p. 107). The 6-man Polish crew were killed. On 14 September 1942 a Bristol Beaufighter suffered engine trouble and crashed on farmland near Penmynydd. The aircraft burst into flames and was completely destroyed. There were no fatalities. On 26 September 1942 a Hawker Henley (from RAF Bodorgan) crashed at Tŷ Croes, resulting in the death of both crewmen. One of them is buried in the cemetery at St Cadwaladr's Church, Llangadwaladr. Again, none of these incidents was reported in the press.

The long-awaited British Restaurant opened in Holyhead on 1 September. It was initially reported to be serving 1,700 meals per week.

Organisers of a 'Tanks for Attack' campaign in Holyhead were initially rebuked for failing to raise sufficient money, but by November had exceeded the target and £3,749 had been raised for the supply of two Churchill tanks. After much deliberation, it was decided to give the tanks the rather mundane name *Holyhead Schools*.

One of the more unusual and innovative aspects of Anglesey wartime life was the Fruit Preservation Scheme organised by the Women's Institute. Members of the WI prepared jam, bottles of fruit, chutney and pickles. It was reported that when the season ended in October 1942, 1,500lb of preserves had been produced by the Llangefni branch.

On Thursday 8 October 1942 a Bristol Beaufighter crashed at the Q-site near Newborough (see Map 3, p. 107). As explained previously (see Chapter 13), this Q-site was a decoy, with runway lights deployed in darkness, the intention being to protect the airfield at Valley. No enemy aircraft ever attacked the site, but on this cloudy night in October 1942 an Australian crew flying the Beaufighter aircraft (stationed at Valley) were taking part in night exercises. Because one of the aircraft's engines failed, the pilot decided to return to Valley immediately. Unfortunately, he erroneously concluded that the Q-site landing lights were those of Valley airfield and came in to land at Newborough. The Beaufighter crashed in the sand dunes and burst into flames. The two crewmen (Warrant Officer R.N.B. Scott, aged 20 and Sergeant C.A.G. Wood, aged 21) were killed and were later buried at Maeshyfryd Cemetery, Holyhead.

The graves of the two Australian airmen at Maeshyfryd Cemetery, Holyhead. They died in the Newborough Q-site tragedy of 8 October 1942.

The Q-site remained in use until 1943. By then the number of enemy aircraft in the skies over north-west Wales had declined markedly and it was considered that it was no longer necessary. After the war, from 1948 onwards, trees were planted on Newborough Warren and gradually traces of the Q-site began to disappear – in fact most of it was buried by sand in the 1980s and only a little remains to be seen now.

Meanwhile, at RAF Valley, the sand of Tywyn Trewan continued to cause problems – so much so that it was decided to dredge silt from nearby lakes and spread it over the sandy areas of the airfield. During the dredging operation about 150 important Iron Age artefacts were found in Llyn Cerrig Bach and were taken to the National Museum of Wales in Cardiff. The plan worked well and the problem of wind-blown sand was greatly reduced. The runways at Valley were also being extended to accommodate the large American Flying Fortress aircraft. Britain and the USA were making use of these heavy bombers to bomb German cities, the British attacking by night and the Americans by day.

Away from home, severe fighting continued in North Africa and a breakthrough occurred in October 1942 when Montgomery launched a successful offensive against German and Italian troops at El Alamein. By 23 November much territory had been recaptured.

In an unusual court case in Holyhead on 12 November, a woman living in Market Street was imprisoned for 14 days for 'throwing a drawer full of food down the stairs thereby causing waste'. It seems that a domestic incident took place on 18 September and during the quarrel the food was thrown in a fit of temper. The police found sugar, eggs, butter and bacon strewn over the floor. Today we would regard such punishment as unnecessarily severe and totally inappropriate, but the authorities were clearly determined that food was not to be wasted.

Anglesey's War Agricultural Committee issued the island's farmers with quotas for the food they were to produce. The pressure on farmers was intense and some regarded it as unfair, given that the penalties for failing to comply with these orders were severe. In the first case of its kind in Anglesey in November 1942, a Brynsiencyn farmer was ordered to pay £130 in fines and costs for contravening the Agricultural Foodstuffs Order (1942) and for failing to comply with an order made by the Anglesey War Agricultural Committee.

At the end of the year there were vociferous complaints from Holyhead about the 'malicious damage' and 'wanton destruction' to air raid shelters in the town. It seems that considerable damage had been caused but, despite stringent efforts, the perpetrators had not been caught. There was a general feeling that levels of juvenile crime had risen sharply since the beginning of the war and this was common to most areas of Britain.

The authorities were very keen to ensure that the ban on private motoring and the unnecessary use of fuel was strictly enforced. On 18 December two members of the BBC staff at Bangor were returning to Bangor having been to Dwyran, Anglesey, to collect poultry for the private use of BBC staff. They were stopped by a policeman and asked the purpose of their journey. They later appeared in court charged with

Members of Anglesey's War Agricultural Committee on an Anglesey farm.

breaching wartime fuel regulations and fined £5 and £25. Any motorist using the roads could expect to be stopped and questioned about the purpose of their journey; if they were found to be in breach of the regulations, a court appearance and a fine was almost certain.

Another Anglesey airfield, RAF Heneglwys, was constructed in 1942 on a site which had been used for the deployment of airships during the First World War (see Map 5, p. 125). In 1920 Anglesey County Council had bought the site and some of the buildings had been converted into a small isolation hospital (the Druid Hospital). This hospital was now to be transferred to Llangefni. The construction of the airfield involved extending the site by the acquisition of more farmland and the demolition of no fewer than nine smallholdings. The airfield with its three runways was largely complete by summer 1942, but finally opened on 1 December 1942 after the three hangars were completed. Its name was soon changed to RAF Mona and the airfield was largely a training establishment (for gunners and wireless operators) which acquired a number of obsolete Blackburn Botha aircraft from RAF Castle Kennedy, which did not prove popular with aircrews. RAF Mona had a communications centre at a place called Pen y Foel near Llannerch-y-medd where several people were employed. Pen y Foel is over 300ft above sea level and was seen as an ideal location for such an installation. Two structures can still be seen on this site: a now-roofless building which once housed the radio equipment and its operators, and the base on which the radio mast was mounted.

During a 6–7 month period in 1942, parts of the documentary film *Western Approaches* was filmed in and around Holyhead (the remainder of the film was shot at Pinewood Studios). The 83-minute film was produced by the Crown Film Unit and is said to be the first documentary to be shot in colour. It was a tribute to the Merchant Navy and told the story of a merchant vessel struck by a German torpedo in the Atlantic. Several Holyhead people worked as extras in the film, which was photographed by Jack Cardiff, later to become one of Britain's best-known cinematographers. The film was released in 1944. In June 2007 a commemorative plaque to honour the film was unveiled at Holyhead's Maritime Museum.

The Beveridge Report, published in December 1942, was a far-reaching report which had a profound impact on the lives of everyone in Britain after the war years. Lord William Beveridge (1879–63) was an economist and his report formed the basis for the social reform legislation of the Labour government immediately after the war. Beveridge identified five evils that he felt needed to be tackled: illness, ignorance, want, disease and squalor. Lord Beveridge proposed that all people of working age should make a weekly contribution (National Insurance) which could then be used to benefit the sick and unemployed. It has to be borne in mind that pre-war Britain was still a society divided by class and that the differences between the privileged classes and the working class were enormous.

CHAPTER FIFTEEN

1943

The new year started in Anglesey on an optimistic note. Anglesey County Council noted that the new isolation hospital (transferred from Mona) was due for completion in the very near future and that a site had been found for the previously discussed milk factory. The provision of school meals and the vaccination of children against disease was also discussed and the council was also keen to improve the water supply on the island. There was little doubt that by this time local government was looking ahead to the post-war period.

An organisation known as the Anglesey Ladies' Comforts Committee knitted various items (which they called 'comforts') for members of the forces. It was reported that during 1942 a total of 6,276 items had been received into the County Depot.

On 10 January a Bristol Beaufighter based at RAF Valley crash landed after striking a house at Cemaes during a military exercise. There were no casualties. On 25 January 1943 a de Havilland Mosquito (also from RAF Valley) came down during the night near the railway line. The crew were unhurt, but a train hit some wreckage. On Monday 1 February 1943 a Handley Page Halifax (with a crew of 8) crashed near Four Mile Bridge due to engine failure (see Map 3, p. 107). There were no survivors and five of the crew were Canadians; they were buried at Holyhead.

In wartime Britain there was an endless stream of appeals, often for money but also for other commodities. During the fortnight 6–20 February a book appeal, organised by the Ministry of Supply, was held. The public was urged to hand in any unwanted books or periodicals which would then be used by members of the armed forces or be sent to bombed libraries in other parts of Britain. As always with wartime appeals a target was set, but locally this was exceeded.

On 12 February 1943 the Ellerman Line's SS *Castilian* was hit by a severe storm in Porth Swtan (Church Bay) and she ran on to the East Platters (near the Skerries) where she wedged (see Map 6, p. 136). Fortunately the crew of 47 were rescued by Holyhead lifeboat by repeatedly taking the lifeboat alongside until everyone was saved. A few hours later the *Castilian* sank in 100ft of water, taking her cargo of copper ore and explosives with her. We have to remember that lighthouses were less bright during the war and although the Skerries lighthouse was nearby, the lack of light may have contributed to this disaster. Two members of the Holyhead lifeboat crew, Coxwain Richard Jones and mechanic John Jones, were each awarded the RNLI bronze medal for bravery.

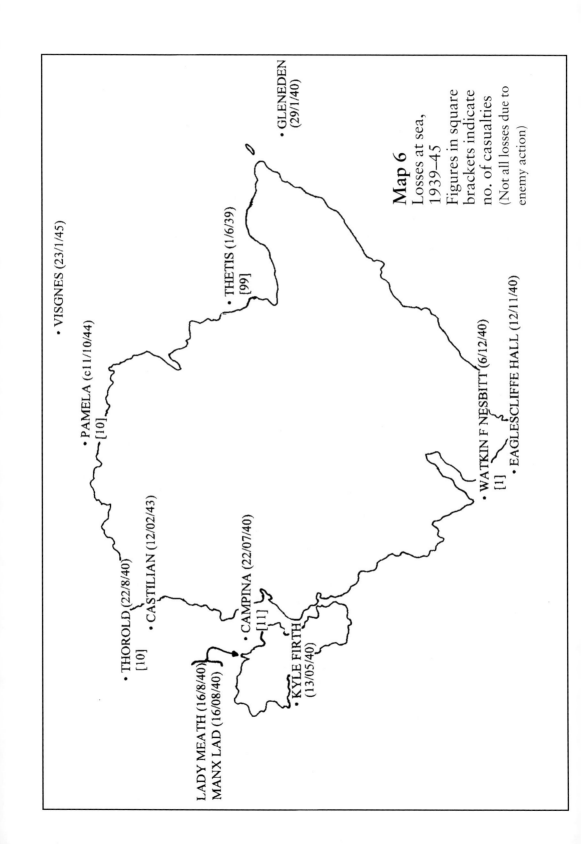

VISGNES (23/1/45)

PAMELA (c11/10/44)
[10]

THOROLD (22/8/40)
[10]
• CASTILIAN (12/02/43)

LADY MEATH (16/8/40)
MANX LAD (16/08/40)

CAMPINA (22/07/40)
[11]

KYLE FIRTH
(13/05/40)

GLENEDEN
(29/1/40)

THETIS (1/6/39)
[99]

WATKIN F NESBITT (6/12/40)
[1]
• EAGLESCLIFFE HALL (12/11/40)

Map 6
Losses at sea,
1939–45
Figures in square
brackets indicate
no. of casualties
(Not all losses due to
enemy action)

The new Isolation Hospital (the Druid Hospital) was opened in Llangefni on 18 March. It was located on the western outskirts of the town. It remained there for many years until its closure in 1989.

In April a further budget imposed increases in the duty on beers, wines, spirits and tobacco but personal taxation was not increased. Purchase tax on luxury items was increased to 100 per cent. Even in wartime with so many people living in impoverished circumstances, there were obviously people who could afford such goods.

Also in April Mr James Griffiths (MP for Llanelli) gave a talk in Anglesey on 'Post War Wales'. This reflected a spirit of optimism that the Allied campaign was bearing fruit and that end of the war might be in sight. In fact Mr Griffiths suggested that the war might be over in two years or possibly in as little as a few months! It is interesting to note that James Griffiths went on to become a successful politician and was the first Secretary of State for Wales when the Welsh Office was established in 1964.

It was reported in April that the submarine *Thunderbolt* was lost in action. The vessel had been previously known as the *Thetis* in which 99 people lost their lives in 1939 (see p. 92).

In May there were events organised to celebrate the third anniversary of the formation of the Home Guard. There were parades and displays in all parts of Anglesey. Further afield in the same month the RAF carried out the famous 'dambuster' raids on dams in the Rühr Valley; they used the famous 'bouncing bombs' devised by Sir Barnes Wallis.

Among the more bizarre money-raising efforts of the war was the 'Bombs for Germany' campaign announced in May. The public were invited to stick savings stamps on bomb cases which would later be filled with high explosives and dropped on German targets. Another appeal held in 1943 was the 'Wings for Victory' campaign. This followed the War Weapons Week of 1941 and the Warship Week of 1942. The Anglesey Wings for Victory campaign was held between 29 May and 5 June and, as before, each area of the island was given a target sum; the total target for Anglesey was £300,000: a target considerably less than the previous year's Warship Week. The campaign week involved the usual events, such as pageants and processions, military and naval bands, dances, concerts, displays, exhibitions and competitions. The campaign was successful and the target was exceeded; Anglesey's total was £428,471.

By mid-1943 German aircraft activity was much reduced; the Allies were very much in control of the air and the war had turned very much in the Allies' favour. RAF Valley was to take on a new responsibility as a transatlantic terminal for the huge bombers of the American 8th Air Force as they flew from the United States to bomb Germany. These heavy bombers came over in great numbers and became a familiar sight in the skies above Anglesey for the remainder of the war.

During the summer of 1943, the unpopular Blackburn Botha aircraft at RAF Mona were replaced by Avro Ansons which proved more popular and useful. Later in the year No. 8 (Observers) Advanced Flying Unit took over Mona. They trained RAF

The remains of one of the buildings at Pen y Foel, Llannerch-y-medd. This was used as a communications centre for RAF Mona.

Observers in other areas such as navigation, gunnery and wireless operation. They also trained in the skill of bomb aiming; practice targets were located at a small site at Lligwy (near Moelfre). This continued until 1945.

The Allies believed that the ultimate defeat of Germany could only be achieved with a foothold in Western Europe. Consequently they invaded Sicily in July 1943 and by early September 1943, British and Canadian forces landed at the 'toe' of Italy. Italy was in turmoil as Mussolini had been deposed and arrested in July 1943. The Germans fought on, but were gradually forced northwards. The new Italian Government, under Marshal Badoglio, declared war on Germany.

On the afternoon of Monday 19 July 1943 an extraordinary piece of bad luck resulted in the deaths of three innocent civilians. A Vickers Wellington bomber, on a training exercise over Anglesey, suffered a failure of both engines. The crew of four bailed out and all but one survived. The aircraft would inevitably crash somewhere but the crew hoped that it would come down in the sea – even if it crashed onto a sparsely populated rural part of Anglesey, there was always the possibility that no deaths or damage to property would result. In fact, the aircraft went on to crash onto a field near Llanfigael (not far from Llanddeusant), burst into flames and then ploughed through a hedge and on to a country road before colliding with a car and setting it alight (see Map 3, p. 107). The car was driven by Dr Mark William Chill (aged 64), a general practitioner who lived at Trygarn, Bodedern. The doctor was on his rounds and he was accompanied by his wife Marjorie (aged 30) and his mother-in-law Mary Scott (aged 73). At an inquest, Grace M. Pritchard, who lived near the scene of the crash, stated that she saw a man with his clothes on fire. The man pleaded with her to look for his wife and mother-in-law. In fact, both women were dead at the scene of the crash. Dr Chill was taken to hospital where he died the following day. Dr Chill and his wife were buried at Bodedern. The coroner described the incident as a million to one chance and recorded a verdict of accidental death. It is ironic that these civilian deaths in wartime Anglesey would be caused by a British aircraft.

The National Eisteddfod was to have been held in Llangefni in August 1943, however, in view of wartime travel restrictions and rationing, it was felt that it should be held in a more easily reached location. Consequently the Eisteddfod was relocated to Bangor in the first week of August 1943.

On 21 August 1943 an Avro Anson ditched in the sea near Point Lynas (on the north-east tip of Anglesey) while on a night exercise. Thanks to the efforts of the Amlwch Royal Observer Corps, the crew of five were rescued. The Royal Observer Corps played a very important role during the war. If enemy aircraft were spotted, the information was relayed to an Interception Centre so that Allied aircraft could pursue and destroy the intruders.

In early September Anglesey County Council decided to promote a bill in parliament to give them powers to implement a water supply scheme. This came as a result of the Rafferty Report which was published following an extensive review of the county's water supply. Also in September, over 100 relatives of Anglesey men held as prisoners of war attended a meeting in Bangor. The meeting was organised by the Holyhead Prisoners of War Relatives' Association. Those who attended were given an insight into life in a German camp – the purpose of the meeting was to reassure the relatives that life in enemy hands, while not pleasant, was tolerable.

There was concern in Anglesey at this time over the lack of train services. Naturally, the railway companies were expected to give priority to war transport and as a result passenger services had deteriorated. Holyhead residents were especially concerned at the lack of trains in the morning. After the first train left Holyhead at 6.55 a.m., the next did not depart until 10.45 a.m., so the LMS railway company were being urged to schedule a train between the two. A further irritation was that some trains left Holyhead empty and were not allowed to pick up passengers until they reached Valley; on their return passengers alighted at Valley and the trains proceeded empty to Holyhead. Wartime regulations could sometimes be very irksome and inflexible; people were generally very patient, but sometimes their patience could be tried to the limit.

An example of wartime inflexibility and lack of common sense reached the Holyhead courts in early October 1943. A 16-year-old girl working in a Holyhead grocery shop charged a customer 7½d per pound for a cauliflower instead of the regulation price of 5d. She claimed that her employers had instructed her to charge this price. The magistrates commented that the shop proprietor should have been before the court, not the assistant.

The Moelfre lifeboat took part in a number of wartime rescues, including the Gleneden incident in 1940 and the rescue of airmen near Ynys Dulas in 1943.

The memorial to Richard Evans (1905–2001) near the Sea Watch Centre, Moelfre. Evans was a crew member of the Moelfre lifeboat during the Second World War and took part in some notable rescues during that period.

The case against the girl was dismissed, while the following month the shop owner did appear in court charged with the same offence. He was found guilty and fined £10.

On 18 October 1943 a Bristol Beaufighter (based at Valley) crashed at Tŷ Croes after breaking up in mid-air, killing the pilot (see Map 3, p. 107). The incident was not reported in the local press.

In the early hours of 21 October an Armstrong Whitworth Whitley aircraft suffered engine failure and ditched into the sea near Ynys Dulas, north of Moelfre. The four-man crew were able to scramble into a dinghy and were rescued by Moelfre lifeboat in appalling weather conditions. The coxswain John Matthews received an RNLI silver medal and bronze medals were awarded to crew members Richard Evans and Robert Williams. Each member of the crew received a reward of £4 17s 6d.

In early November Robert T. Jones, a seaman in the Merchant Navy who had been held as a prisoner for 3½ years, was repatriated and returned to his home in Gilbert Street, Holyhead. His vessel had been attacked by German naval units and he was held prisoner in Norway, Denmark and later in Germany, in an internment camp for merchant seamen. He was released and allowed to travel to Sweden before returning to Liverpool. He claimed that the Germans 'know they're beaten' and were hoping that the Allies would reach them before the Russians. Robert Jones was given a civic welcome by the town council. Repatriations of this type were fairly uncommon, but we have to remember that merchant seamen were not part of the armed forces and therefore not technically prisoners of war. In the same month, a Llangefni man, Owen Jones, was repatriated also after 3½ years in an internment camp.

On 9 November 1943 a de Havilland Tiger Moth (from RAF Bodorgan) crashed at Llangaffo. Both crewmen were killed. The cause of the crash was unauthorised low flying. On 22 November 1943 a Bristol Beaufighter ditched in the sea off Holyhead, killing two of the crew (see Map 3, p. 107).

From December 1943 onwards, young British men were conscripted to work in the country's coal mines. These became known as Bevin Boys. A certain proportion (10 per cent) of conscripts aged 18–25 were picked for this purpose as the coal industry had suffered greatly when many of its key workers were conscripted into the armed forces. The scheme lasted for the duration of the war and beyond. The Bevin Boys received no medals and were not given the right to return to the jobs they previously held (unlike conscripts in the armed forces). The Bevin Boys finally received a commemorative badge for their efforts in March 2008.

CHAPTER SIXTEEN

1944

The new year saw a new mood of optimism concerning the progress of the war and increasingly there was talk of development plans for Anglesey after the war ended. One piece of good news was the opening of the much-discussed and eagerly awaited milk factory in Llangefni on 1 January. It was officially opened by Megan Lloyd George MP on 2 March and was one of only a few factories opened in Britain during the war that did not supply the war effort. There were 400 producers supplying the factory and initially about 90 per cent of its production was taken to Merseyside.

In mid-January the Anglesey Council Comforts Committee appealed for scarves, caps, gloves and mittens for the use of troops. The committee supplied wool free from the County Depot in Llangefni to registered parties who were prepared to knit the items required.

Aircraft accidents continued and there were three involving fatalities early in the year (see Map 3, p. 107). On 29 January 1944 an Avro Anson (from RAF Mona) crashed at Llannerch-y-medd killing one of the crew; the other four survived. Just over a week later on 8 February 1944 a Miles Martinet (from RAF Bodorgan) crashed at Gorsgoch, Holyhead, killing the pilot. Unauthorised low flying was blamed. On 20 February 1944 a Bristol Beaufighter (from RAF Crosby) made an emergency landing at RAF Valley. The crew were killed instantly.

Local councils on the island were beginning to discuss the building of war memorials after the end of the conflict. Menai Bridge Council discussed whether a town hall might be a fitting memorial, but one councillor suggested a cottage hospital. Holyhead Council considered the building of a memorial hall, but also discussed the possibility of making a cash grant to each serving man or woman on their return.

The provision of a water supply for the island's residents was further discussed by the County Council in March. It was stated that only the urban areas and five of the island's villages had mains water. All the other villages and rural areas were dependent on wells and other means of supply; in fact only one-third of the island was adequately supplied. The Anglesey County Council (Water) Act would be passed by parliament later in the year.

On 3 March 1944 a Blackburn Botha (from RAF Hooton Park) came down in the sea near the Skerries (see Map 3, p. 107). Two of the four-man crew were rescued; the other two died.

The hall of the Presbyterian Chapel in Caergeiliog was used by the RAF as an operations room for Valley airfield for a time during the Second World War.

On 10 March the Education Act was passed. It raised the school leaving age to 15 and was Britain's education blueprint for many years to come. Later in the same month, the *Chronicle* reported rumours that the 300-year-old Beaumaris Grammar School was to be moved; the town council sent Anglesey County Council a resolution condemning any such proposal.

The major war fundraising scheme for 1944 was to be known as the 'Salute the Soldier' campaign. In Anglesey it was held in the week 3–10 June. As before, each area was given a target amount, and the total target for the island was again set at £300,000. The week involved the usual parades, exhibitions, dances and other events and turned out to be a great success, raising £435,387 – well in excess of the target. The total for the North Wales counties was £6,792,565. The D-Day landings by British and American troops in Normandy occurred during this campaign week and would certainly have boosted morale and may possibly have helped the fundraising.

On 13 June, less than a week after D-day, the south-east of England faced a new horror – the first of the V1 flying bombs (Vergeltungswaffe eins or 'doodlebugs' as they became known). They were launched from fixed launch sites in German occupied Europe but were never a threat to Anglesey or indeed to most of the United Kingdom because of their limited range, but their sinister sound and destructive power caused terror in London and the south-east of England. In fact in August, 176 evacuated women and children from Kent and the south-east of England arrived at Holyhead. Far fewer German aircraft entered British airspace at this point in the war, but the evacuation was necessary because of the V1 flying bombs. The evacuees were billeted to various addresses in Holyhead.

In July an appeal was launched to raise £100,000 for the provision of additional buildings and facilities at the Caernarfonshire and Anglesey (C and A) Hospital at Bangor. This hospital (the site of which is now occupied by the Morrisons supermarket) was the forerunner of Ysbyty Gwynedd and the general hospital for the people of Anglesey. The appeal ran for the duration of the war and well beyond.

On 20 July 1944 a group of German officers attempted to assassinate Adolf Hitler. A bomb was placed and when it exploded it killed five people but Hitler himself was only slightly injured. The conspirators were executed. This was a sure sign that there were those, even in the highest ranks of the German war machine, who felt that the war was lost and that it was pointless to continue, but continue it would, for the best part of a year.

On 2 September 1944 a US Air Force Douglas C-47 Dakota made an emergency landing at Valley with one engine on fire. The engine came off just before landing and fell near Rhosneigr Golf Club. The aircraft then crash-landed and was destroyed by fire, though fortunately the crew were uninjured.

On a lighter note, during September the *Chronicle* reported that Corporal Idris Williams of Menai Bridge, serving with the RAF in North Africa, had met a Welsh-speaking Arab. It seems that the Arab had worked in Cardiff docks for 17 years and had acquired the language there! In the same month Holyhead Town Council paid tribute to the gallantry of Jack Everett. He was reported to have escaped from a prisoner of war camp in Italy and rejoined his unit. Such stories always went down well in wartime.

On 8 September 1944 the V2 rockets began being launched against London and the south-east of England. These rockets (the world's first ballistic missiles) were launched from mobile launch sites and had a range of approximately 200 miles, thus most of the United Kingdom was beyond their range. The public remained in the dark about their nature for some two months.

On 17 September relaxations in the blackout regulations came into force as German aerial activity was much reduced. Now ordinary curtains were deemed to be sufficient and only skylights needed to be completely blacked out. There was also an easing of restrictions for bikes but not for car headlamps, although some street lamps could also be lit; those at Holyhead were switched on again exactly 40 years after the town was lit by electricity for the first time in 1904. These concessions would have been seen by the general public as a morale-booster and a sign that the conflict was in its final stages.

In September Anglesey Education Committee announced that a site had been chosen for a new secondary school at Amlwch. It was also announced that 629 evacuees were continuing to receive their education on the island. It seems that a number had returned to their homes and that others would soon leave – a relief for many – the presence of evacuees was a considerable burden as well as a source of tension.

At a Holyhead court in September an Austrian named Hendrich Hans Josef Mosser, classed as an 'enemy alien', was jailed for three months for disregarding wartime restrictions. He was said to have changed address without permission and to have travelled further than permitted. He had served in the German navy from 1939 to 1942 and claimed that he was in Holyhead because he intended to travel to Ireland.

On 10 October 1944, the 408-ton coaster *Pamela*, belonging to the Anglesey Shipping Company, set sail from Sharpness (on the River Severn in Gloucestershire) to Liverpool with a cargo of 350 tons of barley. The ship never reached her destination and was never seen again. It was presumed that the ten men aboard (eight crew and two gunners) had died. Some weeks later a wooden plank bearing the word 'Pamela' was found in Red Wharf Bay. An inquiry into the ship's disappearance, held in 1947, considered various options but was unable to establish an exact cause, though it was considered likely that drifting mines were the most likely reason for the ship's disappearance. The location of the *Pamela* remained a mystery for decades until divers discovered the wreck off the Anglesey coast (about 5 miles north of Amlwch) in the late 1990s (see Map 6, p. 136).

With increasing talk of an end to hostilities there was some concern and even anger that wartime restrictions were not being further eased. A *Chronicle* editorial in October commented that 'Government Departments are determined to maintain the burdens on the backs of the people to the last moment. We should expect a little comfort now'.

Winston Churchill had led the wartime coalition government since 1940. With the end of the war now a real prospect, there were inevitably demands for an early general election. In November Churchill declared that it would probably be 7–9 months before an election could be held. In Anglesey, 28-year-old Cledwyn Hughes, then serving in the RAF, was chosen as Anglesey's Labour candidate for the general election. He was the son of the Revd H.D. Hughes, minister of Disgwylfa Presbyterian Chapel, Holyhead. Cledwyn Hughes, of course, went on to become one of Wales' foremost politicians, eventually entering the House of Lords as Lord Cledwyn of Penrhos.

In Holyhead concern was expressed that the public were not allowed onto the platform at Holyhead railway station – only travellers were permitted to be there. This restriction had been in place for some time and the town council were keen for it to be removed. It was also announced in November that the Crosville Motor Company intended to use double-decker buses on the Bangor to Holyhead route in the near future.

On 1 December the Home Guard stood down after 4½ years. The threat of invasion posed by the Germans had receded so much that they were no longer considered necessary, although the Home Guard organisation itself remained in place in case they were needed again. The Anglesey Home Guard conducted their final parade in Holyhead on Sunday 3 December.

On 22 December 1944 an American Consolidated Liberator aircraft (known as the Jigs Up), having been diverted to Valley due to bad weather, ran out of fuel near North Stack (see Map 3, p. 107). The crew of ten parachuted from the doomed aircraft; the pilot and co-pilot survived but the other eight died. They are presumed to have drowned although their bodies were never found. There has been a memorial to those who lost their lives in this tragedy in the Breakwater Country Park at Holyhead since 1993.

The memorial in the Breakwater Country Park, Holyhead, for the eight men who drowned when an American Liberator aircraft ran out of fuel near North Stack on 22 December 1944.

With the end of the war seemingly in sight there was increasing talk of 'Welcome Home Committees' and 'Welcome Home Funds' in the island's towns and villages. Various events, such as concerts and dances, were organised. At a concert in Beaumaris in December, the Talwrn Children's Choir performed. This choir, established and conducted by Cecil Jones, became quite famous during the war and performed all over Britain at literally hundreds of concerts. It was reported that the choir raised £7,000 for various charities.

In his Christmas broadcast for 1944, King George VI proclaimed that 'the lamps of Europe are being rekindled'. It was everyone's hope that 1945 should finally see the end of the war. However, the year ended with a particularly unpleasant incident at Holyhead. On 26 December there was a shooting on board a coastal vessel docked at the port which led to the death of a 27-year-old Irish woman called Annie Mulkarrins. A nineteen-year-old Birkenhead man, James Eric Holmes, was charged with murder.

CHAPTER SEVENTEEN

1945

On 1 January 1945 Anglesey County Council became its own water authority under the 1944 Act. Anglesey was the only authority throughout Wales and England to undertake such a responsibility. The Act enabled Anglesey County Council to take over the Holyhead Water Company, a number of public wells and to build new reservoirs.

In the New Year Honours List David Lloyd George was made an earl, taking the title Earl Lloyd George of Dwyfor. His daughter Megan Lloyd George, MP for Anglesey throughout the war, became Lady Megan Lloyd George. David Lloyd George died less than three months later and was buried at Llanystumdwy.

The *Chronicle* editorial in the issue dated 5 January was in less optimistic mood. It declared that 'the victory that appeared within our grasp has receded'. The public were understandably frustrated that six months after D-Day and after the campaign to liberate Europe had initially gone well, the Germans were providing surprisingly strong resistance in some areas and the progress towards their defeat was proving painfully slow.

The Anglesey newspapers were carrying appeals for household goods (mundane items such as brooms, doormats and clocks) for people in London and the south-east of England who had lost everything in attacks by V1 and V2 rockets. Because of wartime shortages such items were almost impossible to obtain in the shops.

On 15 January, the 8,080-ton merchant vessel *Maja* was torpedoed and sunk by German submarine U-1055 with the loss of 24 lives. The attack occurred in the Irish Sea midway between Anglesey, the Isle of Man and the Irish coast while the vessel was en route from Swansea to Belfast and then Reykjavik. Forty survivors were picked up by the Dutch coaster *Hendrik Conscience* and landed at Holyhead. Some of the dead were taken to the Isle of Man for burial, while others were buried at Maeshyfryd Cemetery, Holyhead; the gravestones bear Chinese names.

On 23 January, the 1,600-ton Norwegian-owned steamship *Visgnes*, which was carrying 2,000 tons of coal from Cardiff, was struck by a torpedo off northern Anglesey (see Map 6, p. 136). It is believed that the German submarine U-1172 may have been responsible. The *Visgnes* sank but the crew of 25 were able to use the ship's lifeboats and they came ashore safely near Point Lynas. The wreck, which is fairly intact and has been extensively examined by divers, lies about 12 miles north-east of Point Lynas.

With the end of the war expected sometime during the year, fundraising activities for welcoming service people home were in full swing in all parts of Anglesey. Events such as concerts, dances, tombolas and whist drives were being held around the island and the Beaumaris fund topped £3,000 in February 1945. It was decided to give an equal cash gift to every male and female who had been in the Army, Navy, Royal Air Force or merchant navy. In Menai Bridge it was decided to hold a plebiscite to determine what was to be done with the money collected. Llanfair Pwllgwyngyll was aiming at a target of £2,000.

Meanwhile, between 4–12 February, the 'Big Three' conference began at Yalta, a Soviet holiday resort in the Crimea. Winston Churchill, Franklin D. Roosevelt and Joseph Stalin represented Britain, the USA and the Soviet Union respectively, and the purpose of the conference was to complete plans for the defeat of Germany and discuss the formation of the United Nations.

A post-war development report was discussed in Holyhead at a council meeting on 20 February. With the end of the war in sight, everyone was keen to see industries established in the area during the war continue to provide employment in peacetime.

By 6 March 1945 the German city of Cologne was captured by the Allies. Germany was overrun within a few weeks and the Allied troops encountered gruesome evidence of the barbarity at Belsen, Buchenwald and other concentration camps. With Allied troops now controlling large parts of Germany, there was a gloomy announcement in mid-March that rationing might have to continue for some time after the war. This was not the sort of thing that the long-suffering British people wished to hear.

Later in the same month the BBC announced that Welsh regional programmes would be resumed within three months of the end of hostilities. The wavelength (373.1 metres on the medium wave) had been used for other purposes since the start of the war. Welsh radio programmes were actually broadcast again after five years on 27 July.

The last V2 rocket landed on 27 March and the last V1 flying bomb was deployed on 29 March. After months of terror in the south-east of England, the wartime aerial bombardment finally came to an end.

The Crosville Motor Company finally started to use double-decker buses on the Bangor-Llangefni-Holyhead route on 1 April. This was made possible by the strengthening of the Menai Suspension Bridge which was completed in 1941. Previously the bridge was subject to a 4¼-ton weight restriction where the normal practice had been for passengers to get off the bus which would then cross the bridge empty and wait for the passengers on the other side!

There is evidence that enemy U-boats were still active in waters not far from Anglesey even at this late stage in the war. The U-1051 was located by a hunting group of four ships (*Aylmer*, *Bentinck*, *Calder* and *Manners*) and was sunk in January (with the loss of the 47-man crew) at the location 53.29N, 5.23W. The U-246 was sunk on about 5 April with the loss of 48 crew. The loss of this submarine is something of a mystery since no allied ship ever claimed to have attacked or sunk her, however, the remains of U-246 have been discovered midway between Anglesey and the Isle of Man at 53.40N, 4.53W. On 12 April, U-1024 was forced to surface by Royal Navy ships *Loch Glendhu* and *Loch More*, and the submarine was attacked by gunfire. The Royal Navy boarded the submarine and took the Enigma code machine from it. U-1024 had a crew of 46, of whom 9 died and 37 were taken prisoner. The following day the Royal Navy attempted to tow the submarine to Liverpool, but the attempt failed when the badly damaged U-1024 sank at 53.39N, 5.03W.

In April it was reported that Holyhead Council were optimistic that the War Damage Commission would pay for repairs to Church House, badly damaged by German bombing in 1940.

Although the war was not officially over, Allied troops were liberating prisoner of war camps in different parts of Germany and a trickle of British prisoners were gradually making their way home. Holyhead's first prisoner of war returned to the UK on 24 April. He was John Victor Jones (aged 25) of 8 Cross Street. He was held at the prison camps of Stalag XXA and Stalag XXB for a total of 5 years. Street banners were in place to welcome him and Holyhead held a welcome home dinner for Jones and other former prisoners on 5 June, although not all of Holyhead's prisoners of war had returned home by then.

In Moelfre, Hugh Parry Jones (aged 29) of Glasfor, who had served with the Welsh Guards, arrived home at the end of April having been a prisoner of war for several months following his capture in Italy. Captain Ivor J. Griffith of Bryn Dulas, Moelfre,

Hugh Parry Jones of Moelfre was one of the first prisoners of war to return home.

also returned home. Both were welcomed at a reception at Capel Carmel schoolroom on 25 May where they gave accounts of what life was like in a German prisoner of war camp. It seems that Captain Griffith had kept a wartime log and one of the camps where he was held was visited by Lord Haw-Haw!

The Russians were advancing on Germany from the east as the Allies advanced towards Berlin from the south and west. As the grip on Germany tightened and defeat for the Nazis was inevitable, Hitler committed suicide in his Berlin bunker on 30 April. The papers were quick to report the news; there was an immense sigh of relief and it heralded the imminent end of the conflict in Europe. German forces capitulated officially a few days later. The war against Japan in the Far East, however, showed no sign of ending.

On 8 May VE Day (Victory in Europe day) was celebrated. In all parts of Anglesey there were street parties, thanksgiving services and many other events. In Aberffraw, the villagers gathered in the square and there was singing in the village's Seion Wesleyan Chapel conducted by Llewelyn Jones. The joy was tingled with sadness, however, as three men from the village had been killed in action. There was further sadness in Amlwch, where the VE Day celebrations were marred by the death of 10-year-old John Henry Jones who was run over by a vehicle during a procession.

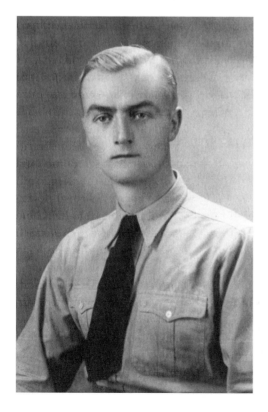

Dyfed Howells was one of many Anglesey servicemen who travelled extensively during the war. Opposite, top: Howells is seen on active service in Italy, 1945.

A Grand VE Dance was held at Plas Newydd near Llanfair Pwllgwyngyll on 24 May where an RAF dance band provided the music; the admission charge to the public was a rather costly 6s.

Holyhead chose 16 May as their date for VE celebration. Children attended a thanksgiving service at Hyfrydle Presbyterian Chapel (in Thomas Street), parades were held in the afternoon and in the evening there were dances, bonfires and fireworks, including the burning of an effigy of Adolf Hitler. The BBC broadcast a programme of hymn-singing from Capel Tabernacl, Thomas Street, on 13 May.

The trickle of prisoners of war was now a flood as more and more returned home on a daily basis, much to the relief of family and friends.

In May the Saunders-Roe company, with their factory just outside Beaumaris, stated that they wished the factory to continue now that the war in Europe was over. This was exactly what Anglesey's civic leaders wanted to hear. The people of Anglesey were keen to see wartime industries continue after the war and they were determined not to return to the pre-war days of recession, unemployment and poverty.

The deployment of RAF Valley by American bombers ended in April 1945 when the aerial bombardment of Germany was coming to an end. Those aircraft then returned home to the United States to be deployed in the war against Japan; Valley was the departure point. The exodus (involving some 2,600 aircraft) was complete by August 1945. Valley's wartime work was then over. Wartime flying at RAF Mona came to an end on 19 May 1945. The aircraft accidents continued despite the cessation of hostilities in Europe. On 16 May an Avro Anson N9911 crashed at RAF Mona (see Map 3, p. 107), where three were killed and one injured. On 20 June a North American P-51 Mustang from RAF Valley crashed in the sea near Valley and the pilot was killed.

On 24 and 25 June a captured German U-boat was on display at Holyhead. The 200ft long U-1023 was on a tour of different ports. It seems that over 5,000 people toured the vessel at Holyhead and £182 was raised for charity.

Air traffic at RAF Bodorgan ceased in August and the base was officially closed in December 1945. For a time some of the buildings were used to house Italian prisoners of war who were working on local farms. Although Italy had changed sides during the war, it had not been possible to repatriate them until after the war ended.

A General Election was held on 5 July. In Anglesey there were only two candidates – Lady Megan Lloyd George (Liberal) and Flying Officer Cledwyn Hughes (Labour), then stationed at RAF Mona. The result of the election was not declared until 27 July in order to allow time for British people abroad to cast their votes. Megan Lloyd George polled 12,610 votes and Cledwyn Hughes polled 11,529 votes, therefore the seat was held by the Liberals as it had been for some years. In Britain as a whole the election was won by the Labour Party and Clement Attlee became prime minister. The wartime coalition government of Conservative, Liberal and Labour under Winston Churchill was over.

The last prisoner of war from Europe to return to Holyhead (Nathaniel William Chambers, aged 26) attended a social evening with other ex-prisoners at Capel Salem, Millbank, Holyhead on 17 July. The Welcome Home Committees in different parts of Anglesey were still working hard to raise money. The Holyhead committee organised a sheepdog trial and an exhibition by British featherweight boxing champion Nel Tarleton during their Appeal Week (4–11 August), while the Llanfair Pwllgwyngyll Committee held a garden fête in the grounds of Plas Llanfair. The Llanddaniel and Llanedwen committee organised a horticultural show, stock sale, bazaar, whist drive and grand dance at Plas Newydd.

At the beginning of August it was reported that the last of the evacuees had left the area and returned home. A few days later, on 15 August, the war against Japan ended (VJ Day) following the deployment of atomic bombs at Hiroshima and Nagasaki resulting in massive loss of life. Japan agreed surrender terms on 14 August 1945. Finally the 2,073-day conflict and its horrors were over. There were celebrations once again in all parts of Anglesey, including services of thanksgiving, street parties and sports events. The following month saw the beginning of the return of prisoners of war who had been held in Japanese hands in the Far East.

A few days after the end of the war the British Government was dismayed to find that the USA was terminating the Lend-Lease Agreement. This scheme had been invaluable to the British people since 1941.

There were increasing calls at this time for men to be released from the armed services as quickly as possible and in sufficient numbers to enable industry to be converted back to peacetime production and expand. The military were also urged to derequisition hotels so that they might be used by the tourist industry. There were suggestions that the Women's Land Army would need to continue for as long as two years after the war in order to provide the country with sufficient food and avoid costly imports.

On 15 September RAF Valley held an open day to enable members of the public to see exhibits including aircraft, workshops, engine repair sheds and so on. The people of Anglesey were finally able to see at first hand what had remained secret throughout the war and an astonishing 7,000 people visited the site.

Slowly but surely, normality was returning to the life of the nation. On 1 October, dining cars made a comeback on LMS trains after the service was suspended in 1943 as an economy measure. It was also announced that the stringent customs examinations which had become the norm at the port of Holyhead were to be eased for British subjects.

In October, it was announced that 50 prefabricated bungalows were to be erected at Holyhead. They were to be allocated to couples with at least two children.

Unfortunately, unlawful activities were still keeping the Anglesey courts busy. In October, two Holyhead women were in court charged with bigamy in order to obtain allowances that they were not entitled to. The judge made the comment 'bigamy is rife'. In the same month five Anglesey men aged between 22 and 30 were charged with stealing a Milk Marketing Board lorry and other vehicles. Three of them were sent to prison for 3 months.

At the end of October, Phyllis Parry who had served as a Nursing Officer in India, Burma and Singapore for four years returned to her home in Station Street, Holyhead. She was given an enthusiastic welcome, having been one of the few Anglesey women on active service in the Far East.

The first peacetime Menai Bridge Fair (Ffair y Borth) since 1938 was held on the usual day; by all accounts it was something of a disappointment, the usual pre-war sparkle was reported to have disappeared.

Although the war was at an end, there was the usual fundraising campaign which had become such a feature of life during the conflict. Clearly the government needed to raise yet more money, this time for rebuilding. The 1945 fundraiser was known as the 'Thanksgiving Campaign' and was held in Anglesey from 27 October to 3 November. Sales of National Savings Certificates and other government investments was once again the intention. The anglesey target was £300,000, which was again exceeded, the total amount raised being £350,839.

The famous Talwrn Children's Choir were reported to have made a recording to be broadcast on short wave to the USA on 2 November. The item included information on the choir's work during the war. Previously the choir members had performed in the Midlands and the north of England in the school holidays and had also broadcast from Dublin.

On 11 November the A.C. Wells company started producing clocks and watches at their factory in Holyhead. This company, originally from London, had produced precision parts for aircraft during the war, but now that the conflict was over, Holyhead Town Council was keen for the factory to remain in order to provide much-needed jobs. The factory owners invested £80,000 and an estimated 500 jobs were promised. The Wells company would be a large employer in Holyhead for many years after the war, producing clocks and later toys and plastic goods at their factory (Progress Works) in Kingsland. In 1945 the plant produced 20,000 clocks a week. The *Chronicle* also reported that a company called Rowley Workshops Ltd wished to establish a furniture factory in a warehouse near Soldiers' Point, Holyhead. This factory was due to start production in January 1946, and would make furniture based on Welsh designs, all for export.

At the end of November a brutal murder took place in Red Wharf Bay. This murder and the subsequent trial of Albert Arthur Nettleton (aged 32) for the murder of his wife were to grab the headlines (both locally and nationally) for weeks.

All parts of Anglesey were keen to see peacetime developments in their own areas. Menai Bridge, for example, was seeking to promote the town for the building of a secondary school and a technical college (for Anglesey and Caernarfonshire).

On 31 December the first shipment of bananas since the beginning of the war reached Britain. This would have been the first time that many small children had seen a banana.

CHAPTER EIGHTEEN

THE AFTERMATH

The population of the United Kingdom was estimated at 47.8 million in 1939. At the end of the war there were approximately 4.75 million men and women in the armed forces. During the war there were an estimated 67,800 civilian deaths (far more than the First World War, largely due to enemy bombing and the V1 and V2 weapons) and 382,600 military deaths (considerably fewer than the First World War). These deaths amounted in total to 0.94 per cent of the population.

In Anglesey there were three civilian deaths during the conflict, but it is estimated that over 300 Anglesey men lost their lives in the armed forces and in the emergency and rescue services. There are 138 names on Holyhead's war memorial alone, representing about 0.77 per cent of Anglesey's population. In general, however, the number of military casualties was lower in the Second World War than in the First World War and the island's war memorials reflect this.

Shortly after the war ended, the British Government gave local communities money to erect war memorials or add plaques to existing First World War memorials. Most communities built memorials listing the names of those who had died in the conflict. In the village of Moelfre, however, the parish council decided that street lighting would be erected to commemorate the dead, and thus, in 1948, Moelfre became the first village in Anglesey to have its streets lit by electricity. It was not until May 2009 that a plaque was unveiled listing the names of the ten Moelfre men who died in the Second World War, with considerable interest being shown in the event by the press and the media.

Moelfre's war memorial featuring the names of ten Merchant seamen.

In February 1946 the County Council was reported to be optimistic about the future of RAF Valley; however, the airbase was declared inactive later in the year and remained so until the 1950s when it became a training establishment. It remains so today and in June 2008 a major investment programme for Valley was announced by the government. Valley is also used as a civilian airport; since 2007 flights between Anglesey and Cardiff have proved popular. On the north-west fringe of the airfield (at Llanfair-yn-neubwll) some wartime buildings can still be seen today. The public are warned to keep clear by signs bearing the words 'MOD Property. Keep Out'. RAF Mona also became redundant but became a relief airfield for RAF Valley. Some wartime buildings can still be seen at Mona and the surrounding area. No use could be found for RAF Bodorgan and the land reverted to agricultural use. Some of the wartime buildings on the site were used for some time by the Bodorgan Estate. Some of these buildings were demolished in the 1990s but some are still standing.

The Tŷ Croes Army Camp continued after the war as an anti-aircraft practice establishment for the Royal Artillery. Guided weapons were tested there from 1951, including the Thunderbird Missile. It later became an RAF radar base (with a large 'golf ball' dome) for a short period. Then, from the mid-1990s, it ceased to be used for military purposes; it is currently used as a motor racing circuit. Some disused military buildings can still be seen on the site.

The Saunders-Roe works at Beaumaris continued after the war. Although demand for flying boats had ceased, the company turned to other engineering work such as the repair and modification of military vehicles and the production of buses. Immediately after the war the reconditioning of old buses was the main activity; 430 people were employed in the plant in April 1946. By September that year the plant began producing new buses. By 1948 the company was a major employer on the island with a workforce of 975 people.

The company continued to be a sizeable employer for a number of years under a variety of names including Cammell Laird and Faun. The Faun company (which manufactures refuse lorries) relocated to modern premises on the Llangefni industrial estate in the 1990s and the Llanfaes factory site is now closed although some buildings (including a few from the wartime period) remain. Thus the Faun factory at Llangefni is a direct legacy of the wartime relocation of Saunders-Roe from the Isle of Wight.

In April 1946, over 200 children of the Bluecoat School (a Liverpool school which had been relocated to Beaumaris in 1939) returned home. Pupils in other schools had returned home many months earlier. Just before they left the area the Bluecoat pupils were taken on a trip around Snowdonia, including the Penrhyn Quarry and Beddgelert. In the Bluecoat School in Liverpool there is a plaque to commemorate the school's stay in Beaumaris during the war. In April 2010 former pupils held a reunion and presented Beaumaris band with a school shield to commemorate the school's association with the band during the Second World War.

At the end of May 1946 the Chief Constable of Anglesey issued a warning to the public regarding dangerous sites (such as bombing ranges, beach minefields and army training areas) which might contain live ammunition or mines. Fifteen such sites with

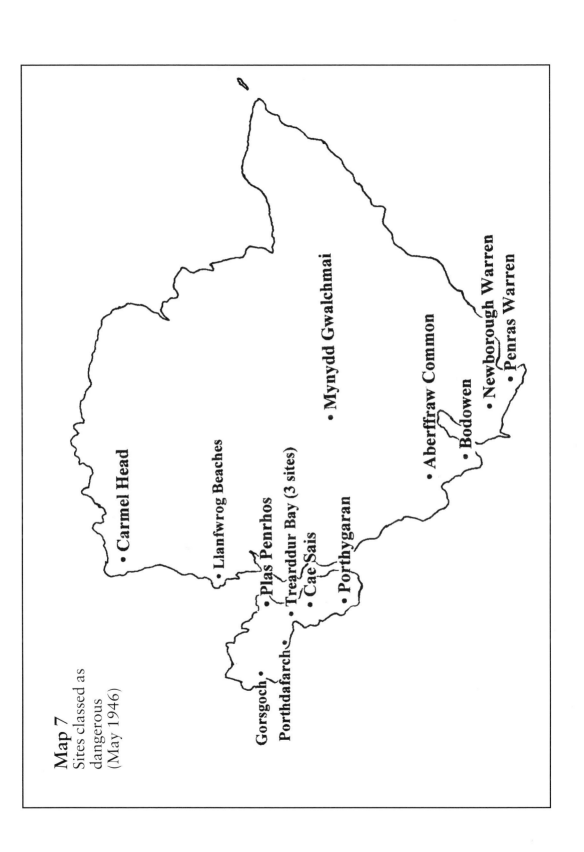

Map 7
Sites classed as
dangerous
(May 1946)

Carmel Head

Llanfwrog Beaches

Plas Penrhos
Trearddur Bay (3 sites)
Cae Sais
Porthygaran

Gorsgoch
Porthdafarch

Mynydd Gwalchmai

Aberffraw Common

Bodowen

Newborough Warren
Penras Warren

a total area in excess of 3,000 acres were identified. Many of these sites (see Map 7, p. 157) were on Holy Island and the south and west coasts.

On 8 June 1946 V-Day was celebrated. This was yet another victory celebration held a year after VE-Day. Holyhead, for example, celebrated with the usual dances, street parties, processions and the crowning of a Victory Queen. It was not as successful as the 1945 celebrations and was not repeated in subsequent years. In Holyhead it was decided that local servicemen would receive a cheque and a 'welcome home' message, printed in Welsh and English, from the Holyhead Welcome Home Committee.

Later in the same month, hopes that Church House, Holyhead (destroyed by enemy bombing in October 1940), could be rebuilt were dashed. The Ministry of Works were not prepared to licence the work (estimated to cost £13,460) because of a shortage of building materials. More urgent work was being given priority.

In August 1946 the LMS railway company placed an order for two new ships for the carrying of passengers and cargo between Holyhead and Dún Laoghaire. These ships would come into service in 1948.

Men who entered war service were entitled to be reinstated in the job they held before being called up. Local Ministry of Labour Reinstatement Committees were established to ensure that, as far as possible, this happened. In September 1939 Richard Williams of Bodorgan appeared before the committee seeking reinstatement as head gardener at Trefeilyr (near Bethel) where he had worked for ten years before joining the forces in July 1941. The Trefeilyr estate claimed that it could not afford to reinstate him, but the committee ordered that he should be given back his old job.

In October 1946 the public were invited to view one of the new prefabricated bungalows in London Road, Holyhead. The prefabs were described as 'all-electric' and were seen as the answer to the area's housing shortage. Llangefni would also have its prefabs; the Bron y Graig estate was built in the late 1940s. It was intended to have only a short life but it actually survived until the 1970s. Conventional housing such as Llangefni's Maes Hyfryd estate was built shortly after the war. In fact, the immediate post-war period saw considerable numbers of council houses built in all parts of Anglesey.

The country as a whole would literally take years to rebuild itself following such a dreadful and costly conflict. In the first two years after the end of hostilities even the elements conspired to hold up Britain's recovery. In autumn 1946 crops were ruined by freak weather conditions and for the first three months of 1947 large parts of Britain were affected by unusually severe snow storms and freezing conditions. Older Anglesey residents will remember the winter weather of 1947 as the worst in living memory. The cold conditions caused a nationwide shortage of coal. In April 1947, when the thaw finally came, there was widespread flooding.

The Beveridge Report entitled 'Social Insurance and Allied Services' had been published in 1942. The Labour Government of 1945–50 acted on this report and this saw the beginning of the welfare state including the National Health Service, family allowances and other benefits.

The grip of rationing was slowly eased from 1945 onwards but did not finally come to an end until 1954, some nine years after the war ended. The last two rationed items were butter and meat.

The Education Act of 1944 enabled Anglesey's Education Committee to take bold steps to reorganise the county's secondary school system. By 1953, Anglesey was the only education authority in Wales and England to establish comprehensive secondary schools.

The Anglesey Water Act of 1944 enabled Anglesey to build a large dam on the River Cefni (west of Llangefni) in order to create a 400 million gallon reservoir to meet all the island's needs for the foreseeable future. Two smaller service reservoirs were also to be built. The County Council voted unanimously in June 1946 to proceed with the scheme at a cost of £668,400, of which £250,000 was provided by the Welsh Board of Health. This major project was completed in April 1951 and it paved the way for all the people of Anglesey to have access to piped water, although it was 1964 before the system was complete.

In Anglesey normality gradually returned. There were fewer servicemen and strangers in the community and aerial activity decreased sharply. Anglesey servicemen returned to their homes, although many would not be demobbed immediately. There were, of course, those who never returned; their names are inscribed on war memorials throughout the island. Some of the refugees who found themselves in Anglesey during the war decided to settle here; even a few evacuees remained and were absorbed into the community.

Anglesey, and the rest of Britain, gradually began to prosper in the 1950s. In 1959 the Prime Minister, Harold Macmillan, famously told the British people, 'You've never had it so good.' This was true; Britons could afford luxuries on a scale they could not have dreamed of before the war and their standard of living had never been higher. But by then the unique wartime community spirit was beginning to weaken.

Two world wars in the space of thirty years had caused massive upheaval in Anglesey and over 1,300 of the island's people lost their lives. Anglesey, in common with the rest of Wales and Britain, saw inevitable changes as a result. The old Anglesey way of life, dominated by agriculture and the chapel, would have to adapt and the island would never be quite the same again.

BIBLIOGRAPHY

Eames, Aled, *Ships and Seamen of Anglesey* (Anglesey Antiquarian Society, 1973)

Gruffydd, Ifan, *Gŵr o Baradwys* (Gwasg Gee, 1963)

Lewis, Keziah Ellen, *Môr a Mynydd* (recollections of life in the Red Wharf Bay and Mynydd Llwydiarth areas)

Lloyd-Hughes, D. and Williams, Dorothy, *Holyhead: The Story of a Port* (Denbigh, 1967)

Looms, Robert R., *Llanddaniel Primary School, Centenary 1874–1974*

Owen, Hugh, *Hanes Plwyf Niwbwrch ym Môn* (Caernarfon, 1952)

Pretty, David, *Anglesey: The Concise History* (University of Wales Press, Cardiff, 2005)

Rees, D. Ben, *John Williams a'i Ddoniau* (Capel Tŷ Rhys, Llangoed, 2009)

Roberts, R.E., *Holyhead and the Great War* (Holyhead, 1920)

Simpson, T.C. *Cnoc ar y Drws* (Llyfrfa'r Methodistiaid Calfinaidd, 1968)

Sloan, Roy, *Anglesey Air Accidents* (Gwasg Carreg Gwalch, 2001)

Williams, William, *Hanes Plwyf Maelog* (Gwasg Carreg Gwalch, 2003)